PENGUIN CLASSICS

CATALOGUE

Notes on Presentation

This catalogue includes every Penguin Classic in print at the time of publication, up to the end of March 2026. Organized alphabetically by author (or by title in the cases of anonymous works and anthologies), it also lists pseudonyms, co-authors, translators and anthology editors. Many works are available in several translations and editions: for example, E. V. Rieu's *Odyssey*, the first Penguin Classics title in 1946, was joined by Robert Fagles' poetic version in the 1990s and by Daniel Mendelsohn's new rendering in 2025; all are listed here, in their various formats, with ISBNs.

When an author has more than one title, these are listed in *alphabetical order*. Where a title exists in more than one translation, these are listed in *chronological order*. If translations appear under different titles, all are included, with prominence given to the most recent.

In general, an author or title's entry follows its presentation on the edition's front cover. Subtitles are included only when they appear on the cover; author names and book titles with diacritical marks also follow the cover presentation.

When a translation has been made by a particularly significant author – for example, Angela Carter's translation of *The Fairy Tales of Charles Perrault* – the book is listed twice, under both original author and translator.

In a few cases, the contents of a single-authored omnibus title are listed in parentheses. This has mainly been done where confusion might otherwise arise; for example, there are two collections by Euripides entitled *Medea and Other Plays*, with different contents. Where a multi-authored anthology includes several standalone novels or plays, these have also been listed in parentheses.

Where titles are published in different formats or sub-series, these are listed in the following order:

1. PC = Penguin Classics (black-spine editions)
2. PMC = Penguin Modern Classics
3. Clothbound = Penguin Clothbound Classics
4. Clothbound Poetry = Penguin Clothbound Poetry
5. HB = Hardback Classics
6. LCC = Little Clothbound Classics
7. Pocket HB = Pocket Hardbacks
8. Demy = Larger 'demy' format for new translations
9. PEL = Penguin English Library
10. Deluxe = Penguin Classics Deluxe Edition
11. Design = Design series
12. Green = Green Ideas
13. Marvel = Penguin Classics Marvel Collection
14. Marvel HB = Penguin Classics Marvel Collection hardback
15. IM = PMC (Inspector Maigret)
16. MCC = Maigret Capsule Collection
17. Great Ideas

18. LBC = Little Black Classics
19. PM = Penguin Modern (mini editions of Penguin Modern Classics)
20. Sci-Fi = Penguin Classics Science Fiction
21. Crime = Penguin Crime and Espionage
22. Westerns = Penguin Westerns
23. Archive = Penguin Archive
24. Student = Penguin Student Readers
25. NS = Non-standard/out of series

A—Z BY AUTHOR

A

ABBEY, EDWARD
The Monkey Wrench Gang
PMC 9780141187624

ABBOTT, EDWIN A.
Flatland: A Romance of Many Dimensions
PC 9780140435313; Sci-Fi 9780241441572

ABE, KOBO
The Ark Sakura
trans. by Juliet Winters Carpenter
Sci-Fi 9780241454589; NS 9780241675304
The Box Man
trans. by E. Dale Saunders
PMC 9780241454596
The Face of Another
trans. by E. Dale Saunders
PMC 9780141188539
The Ruined Map
trans. by E. Dale Saunders
PMC 9780241454602

Secret Rendezvous
    trans. by Juliet Winters Carpenter
    PMC 9780241454619
The Woman in the Dunes
    trans. by E. Dale Saunders
    PMC 9780141188522

ABELARD, PETER
with Héloïse d'Argenteuil
The Letters of Abelard and Heloise
    trans. by Betty Radice
    PC 9780140448993

ACHEBE, CHINUA
Africa's Tarnished Name
    PM 9780241338834
Anthills of the Savannah
    PMC 9780141186900
Arrow of God
    PMC 9780141191560
The Education of a British-Protected Child
    PMC 9780141043616
An Image of Africa
    Great Ideas 9780141192581
A Man of the People
    PMC 9780141186894
No Longer at Ease
    PMC 9780141191553

Things Fall Apart
   PMC 9780141186887; NS 9780141023380

ACKER, KATHY
Blood and Guts in High School
   PMC 9780241302514
Great Expectations
   PMC 9780241352144
New York City in 1979
   PM 9780241338896

ACKERLEY, J. R.
Hindoo Holiday: An Indian Journal
   PMC 9780141189253

ADAMS, NEAL
with Stan Lee, Jack Kirby, Roy Thomas, Werner Roth & Don Heck
X-Men
   Marvel 9780143135777; Marvel HB 9780143135760

ADOMNÁN OF IONA
Life of St Columba
   trans. by Richard Sharpe
   PC 9780140444629

ADONIS

Songs of Mihyar the Damascene
 trans. by Kareem James Abu-Zeid & Ivan Eubanks
 PMC 9780241483558

AESCHYLUS

The Oresteia
 (*Agamemnon, The Libation Bearers, The Eumenides*)
 trans. by Philip Vellacott (as *The Oresteian Trilogy*)
 PC 9780140440676
 trans. by Robert Fagles
 PC 9780140443332
The Persians and Other Plays
 (*The Persians, Prometheus Bound, Seven Against Thebes, The Suppliants*)
 trans. by Philip Vellacott (as *Prometheus Bound and Other Plays*)
 PC 9780140441123
 trans. by Alan H. Sommerstein
 PC 9780140449990
see also *Greek Tragedy*

AESOP

The Complete Fables
 trans. by Robert & Olivia Temple
 PC 9780140446494

African Myths of Origin
    ed. by Stephen Belcher
    PC 9780140449457

The Age of Bede
    trans. by J. F. Webb
    PC 9780140447279

AGEE, JAMES
  A Death in the Family
    PMC 9780141187969
  Let Us Now Praise Famous Men
  with Walker Evans
    PMC 9780141188492

AIRA, CÉSAR
  An Episode in the Life of a Landscape Painter
    Archive 9780241746882

AKUTAGAWA, RYŪNOSUKE
  Hell Screen
    trans. by Jay Rubin
    LCC 9780241573693
  The Life of a Stupid Man
    trans. by Jay Rubin
    LBC 9780141397726
  Rashomon and Seventeen Other Stories
    trans. by Jay Rubin
    PC 9780140449709; Deluxe 9780143039846

ALAIN-FOURNIER, HENRI
The Lost Estate (Le Grand Meaulnes)
trans. by Robin Buss
PC 9780141441894

ALAS, LEOPOLDO
La Regenta
trans. by John Rutherford
PC 9780140443462

ALBERTI, LEON
On Painting
trans. by Cecil Grayson
PC 9780140433319

ALCOTT, LOUISA MAY
Little Men
PEL 9780241652701
Little Women
PC 9780140390698; Clothbound 9780141192413;
PEL 9780241335130; Deluxe 9780143106654
A Merry Christmas and Other Christmas Stories
HB 9780143122463

ALDISS, BRIAN
Hothouse
PMC 9780141189550

ALEICHEM, SHOLOM
:   *Tevye the Dairyman* and *Motl the Cantor's Son*
    :   trans. by Aliza Shevrin
        PC 9780143105602

ALERAMO, SIBILLA
:   *A Woman*
    :   trans. by Erica Segre & Simon Carnell
        PMC 9780241345726

ALEXIEVICH, SVETLANA
:   *Boys in Zinc*
    :   trans. by Andrew Bromfield
        PMC 9780241264119
    Chernobyl Prayer
    :   trans. by Anna Gunin & Arch Tait
        PMC 9780241270530
    Last Witnesses: Unchildlike Stories
    :   trans. by Richard Pevear & Larissa Volokhonsky
        PMC 9780141983561
    The Unwomanly Face of War
    :   trans. by Richard Pevear & Larissa Volokhonsky
        PMC 9780141983530

Alfred the Great: Asser's Life of King Alfred *and Other Contemporary Sources*
:   trans. by Simon Keynes & Michael Lapidge
    PC 9780140444094

AL-HAKIM, TAWFIQ
Return of the Spirit
trans. by William Maynard Hutchins
PC 9780143133971

ALI, SABAHATTIN
Madonna in a Fur Coat
trans. by Maureen Freely & Alexander Dawe
PC 9780241422267

ALLISON, DOROTHY
Bastard Out of Carolina
PMC 9780141391540

AL-NUWAYRI, SHIHAB AL-DIN
The Ultimate Ambition in the Arts of Erudition
trans. by Elias Muhanna
PC 9780143107484

ALPERT, RICHARD
with Timothy Leary & Ralph Metzner
The Psychedelic Experience
PMC 9780141189635

AMADO, JORGE
Captains of the Sands
trans. by Gregory Rabassa
PC 9780143106357

AMBLER, ERIC
   Cause for Alarm
      PMC 9780141190327
   Epitaph for a Spy
      PMC 9780141190310
   Journey into Fear
      PMC 9780141190303; Crime 9780241639177
   A Kind of Anger
      PMC 9780241606179
   The Light of Day
      PMC 9780241606193
   The Mask of Dimitrios
      PMC 9780141190334; Crime 9780241672259
   Passage of Arms
      PMC 9780241606186
   Uncommon Danger
      PMC 9780141190341

American Supernatural Tales
    ed. by S. T. Joshi
    PC 9780143105046; HB 9780143122371

AMIS, KINGSLEY
   The Amis Collection: Selected Non-fiction
      PMC 9780141195308
   The Anti-Death League
      PMC 9780141194295

Collected Poems
　PMC 9780141194219
Complete Stories
　PMC 9780141195292
Difficulties with Girls
　PMC 9780141194226
Ending Up
　PMC 9780141194233
The Folks That Live on the Hill
　PMC 9780141194301
Girl, 20
　PMC 9780141194240
I Want It Now
　PMC 9780141194257
The King's English
　PMC 9780141194318
Lucky Jim
　PMC 9780141182599
New Maps of Hell
　PMC 9780141198620
One Fat Englishman
　PMC 9780141194264
The Riverside Villas Murder
　PMC 9780141049564
Take a Girl Like You
　PMC 9780141194271

That Uncertain Feeling
  PMC 9780141194288

AMMAN, MIR
A Tale of Four Dervishes
  PC 9780140455182

ANAND, MULK RAJ
Coolie
  PMC 9780140186802
Untouchable
  PC 9780141393605

Ancient Rhetoric from Aristotle to Philostratus
  trans. by Thomas Habinek
  PC 9780141392646

ANDERSEN, HANS CHRISTIAN
The Emperor's New Clothes
  trans. by Tiina Nunnally
  Archive 9780241746851
Fairy Tales
  trans. by Tiina Nunnally
  PC 9780140448931; Deluxe 9780143039525;
  HB 9780713996418
The Snow Queen
  trans. by Tiina Nunnally
  LCC 9780241779156

ANDERSON, SHERWOOD
: *Winesburg, Ohio*
: : PC 9780140186550

ANDRADE, MÁRIO DE
: *The Apprentice Tourist*
: : trans. by Flora Thomson-DeVeaux
: : PC 9780143137351

Anecdotes of the Cynics
: trans. by Robert Dobbin
: LBC 9780241251461

ANSELM
: *The Prayers and Meditations of Saint Anselm with the Proslogion*
: : trans. by Benedicta Ward
: : PC 9780140442786

ANSELME, DANIEL
: *On Leave*
: : trans. by David Bellos
: : PMC 9780141977546

The Apocryphal Gospels
: trans. by Simon Gathercole
: PC 9780241340554

APOLLONIUS OF RHODES
Jason and the Argonauts
    trans. by E. V. Rieu (as *The Voyage of Argo*)
    PC 9780140440850
    trans. by Aaron Poochigian
    PC 9780143106869

APPELFELD, AHARON
Badenheim 1939
    trans. by Dalya Bilu
    PMC 9780241681183
Katerina
    trans. by Jeffrey M. Green
    PMC 9780241681190
The Story of a Life
    trans. by Aloma Halter
    PMC 9780241681220

APPIAN
The Civil Wars
    trans. by John Carter
    PC 9780140445091

APULEIUS
The Golden Ass
    trans. by E. J. Kenney
    PC 9780140435900

AQUINAS, THOMAS
Selected Writings
    trans. by Ralph McInerney
    PC 9780140436327

The Arabian Nights: Tales of 1,001 Nights
Tales from the Thousand and One Nights
    trans. by N. J. Dawood
    PC 9780140442892
Tales from 1,001 Nights
    trans. by Malcolm & Ursula Lyons
    PC 9780141191669; Clothbound 9780241382714
Volume 1: Nights 1 to 294
    trans. by Malcolm & Ursula Lyons
    PC 9780140449389
Volume 2: Nights 295 to 719
    trans. by Malcolm & Ursula Lyons
    PC 9780140449396
Volume 3: Nights 719 to 1,001
    trans. by Malcolm & Ursula Lyons
    PC 9780140449402

ARENDT, HANNAH
Eichmann and the Holocaust
    Great Ideas 9780141024004
Eichmann in Jerusalem: A Report on the Banality of Evil
    PMC 9780241552292

The Freedom to Be Free
    Great Ideas 9780241472880
On Violence
    PMC 9780241631645
The Origins of Totalitarianism
    PMC 9780241316757

ARIOSTO, LUDOVICO
Orlando Furioso
    trans. by Barbara Reynolds
    Part One
    PC 9780140443110
    Part Two
    PC 9780140443103

ARISTOPHANES
The Birds and Other Plays
    (*The Knights, Peace, The Birds, Wealth,*
    The Assemblywomen)
    trans. by David Barrett & Alan H. Sommerstein
    PC 9780140449518
The Frogs and Other Plays
    (*The Wasps, The Poet and the Women, The Frogs*)
    trans. by David Barrett
    PC 9780140449693

Lysistrata and Other Plays
   (*The Archarnians*, *The Clouds*, *Lysistrata*)
   trans. by Alan H. Sommerstein
   PC 9780140448146
   see also *Classical Comedy* and *Greek Tragedy*

ARISTOTLE
  The Art of Rhetoric
     trans. by Hugh Lawson-Tancred
     PC 9780140445107
  The Athenian Constitution
     trans. by P. J. Rhodes
     PC 9780140444315
  De Anima (*On the Soul*)
     trans. by Hugh Lawson-Tancred
     PC 9780140444711
  The Metaphysics
     trans. by Hugh Lawson-Tancred
     PC 9780140446197
  The Nicomachean Ethics
     trans. by J. A. K. Thomson, rev. Hugh Tredennick
     PC 9780140449495
     trans. by Adam Beresford
     PC 9780140455472
  One Swallow Does Not Make a Summer
     trans. by J. A. K. Thomson, rev. Hugh Tredennick
     Great Ideas 9780241472866

Poetics
    trans. by Malcolm Heath
    PC 9780140446364
The Politics
    trans. by T. A. Sinclair, rev. Trevor J. Saunders
    PC 9780140444216
see also *Ancient Rhetoric*, *Classical Literary Criticism* and *Greek Tragedy*

ARNOLD, MATTHEW
Culture and Anarchy and Other Selected Prose
    PC 9780141396248

ARPINO, GIOVANNI
Scent of a Woman
    trans. by Anne Milano Appel
    PMC 9780141193182

ARRIAN
The Campaigns of Alexander
    trans. by Aubrey de Sélincourt
    PC 9780140442533

ASKILDSEN, KJELL
Everything Like Before
    trans. by Seán Kinsella
    PMC 9780241508251

ASTURIAS, MIGUEL ÁNGEL
Men of Maize
trans. by Gerald Martin
PC 9780143138402

ATTAR, FARID
The Conference of the Birds
trans. by Afkham Darbandi & Dick Davis
PC 9780140444346

AUGUSTINE
City of God
trans. by Henry Bettenson
PC 9780140448948
Confessions
trans. by R. S. Pine-Coffin
PC 9780140441147; Pocket HB 9780141396897;
Great Ideas 9780141018836

AURELIUS, MARCUS
Meditations
trans. by Martin Hammond
PC 9780140449334; Pocket HB 9780141395869;
Great Ideas 9780141018829
see also *How To Be a Stoic*

AUSTEN, JANE
The Beautifull Cassandra
LBC 9780141397078

The Complete Novels of Jane Austen
  PEL 9780141993744
Emma
  PC 9780141439587; Clothbound 9780141192475;
  HB 9780241804704; PEL 9780141199528;
  Deluxe 9780143107712
The History of England by a Partial, Prejudiced and Ignorant Historian
  Archive 9780241747308
Lady Susan
  LCC 9780241582527; LBC 9780241251331
Lady Susan, The Watsons, Sanditon
  PC 9780140431025
Love and Freindship and Other Youthful Writings
  PC 9780141395111; Clothbound 9780140433340
Mansfield Park
  PC 9780141439808; Clothbound 9780141197708;
  HB 9780241804711; PEL 9780141199870;
  Deluxe 9780143138716
Northanger Abbey
  PC 9780141439792; Clothbound 9780141197715;
  HB 9780241804728; PEL 9780141389424;
  Deluxe 9780143138723
Persuasion
  PC 9780141439686; Clothbound 9780141197692;
  HB 9780241804735; PEL 9780141198835;
  Deluxe 9780143106289

Pride and Prejudice
>   PC 9780141439518; Clothbound 9780141040349;
>   HB 9780241804698; PEL 9780141199078;
>   Deluxe 9780143105428; Deluxe 9780143138730

Sanditon
>   Clothbound 9780241436585; PEL 9780241433713

Sense and Sensibility
>   PC 9780141439662; Clothbound 9780141040370;
>   HB 9780241804681; PEL 9780141199672;
>   Deluxe 9780143106524

AXLINE, VIRGINIA M.
>   *Dibs in Search of Self: Personality Development in Play Therapy*
>   PMC 9780241547977

AYER, A. J.
>   *Language, Truth and Logic*
>   PMC 9780141186047

B

BABEL, ISAAC
Red Cavalry and Other Stories
  trans. by David McDuff
  PC 9780140449976

BACHELARD, GASTON
The Poetics of Space
  trans. by Maria Jolas
  PC 9780143107521

BACHMANN, INGEBORG
Malina
  trans. by Philip Boehm
  PMC 9780241366240

BACON, FRANCIS
The Essays
  PC 9780140432169

BALDWIN, JAMES
Another Country
  PMC 9780141186375

Dark Days
　PM 9780241337547
The Fire Next Time
　PMC 9780140182750; Archive 9780241752388
Giovanni's Room
　PMC 9780141186351; PMC 9780141032948;
　Clothbound 9780241718599
Go Tell It on the Mountain
　PMC 9780141185910
Going to Meet The Man
　PMC 9780140184495
I Am Not Your Negro
　PMC 9780141986678
If Beale Street Could Talk
　PMC 9780140187977
Just Above My Head
　PMC 9780140187991
No Name in the Street
　PMC 9780241711187
Nobody Knows My Name: More Notes of a Native Son
　PMC 9780140184471
Notes of a Native Son
　PMC 9780241334003
Tell Me How Long the Train's Been Gone
　PMC 9780241342039

BALL, JOHN
In the Heat of the Night
PMC 9780241238622

BALZAC, HONORÉ DE
The Black Sheep
trans. by Donald Adamson
PC 9780140442373
Cousin Bette
trans. by Marion Ayton Crawford
PC 9780140441604
Cousin Pons
trans. by Herbert J. Hunt
PC 9780140442052
Eugénie Grandet
trans. by Marion Ayton Crawford
PC 9780140440508
A Harlot High and Low
trans. by Rayner Heppenstall
PC 9780140442328
History of the Thirteen
trans. by Herbert J. Hunt
PC 9780140443011
Lost Illusions
trans. by Herbert J. Hunt
PC 9780140442519

Old Man Goriot
    trans. by Olivia McCannon
    PC 9780140449723
Selected Short Stories
    trans. by Sylvia Raphael
    PC 9780140443257
Ursule Mirouët
    trans. by Donald Adamson
    PC 9780141396705
The Wild Ass's Skin
    trans. by Herbert J. Hunt
    PC 9780140443301

BAMBARA, TONI CADE
The Salt Eaters
    PMC 9780241521380

BARBELLION, W. N. P.
The Journal of a Disappointed Man
    PC 9780241297698

BARBUSSE, HENRI
Under Fire
    trans. by Robin Buss
    PMC 9780141393438

BARDIN, JOHN FRANKLIN
The Deadly Percheron
    Crime 9780241687024

BARRETO, LIMA
The Sad End of Policarpo Quaresma
trans. by Mark Carlyon
PC 9780141395708

BARRIE, J. M.
Peter and Wendy and *Peter Pan in Kensington Gardens*
PC 9780142437933
Peter Pan
PEL 9780241341391

BARTHELME, DONALD
Forty Stories
PMC 9780141180946
Sixty Stories
PMC 9780141180939

BASHO, MATSUO
The Narrow Road to the Deep North
trans. by Nobuyuki Yuasa
PC 9780140441857; Pocket HB 9780241382615
On Love and Barley: Haiku of Basho
trans. by Lucien Stryk
PC 9780140444599
see also *Travels with a Writing Brush*

BASILE, GIAMBATTISTA
The Tale of Tales
trans. by Nancy L. Canepa
PC 9780143129141

BASSANI, GIORGIO
Behind the Door
trans. by Jamie McKendrick
PMC 9780141192130
The Garden of the Finzi-Continis
trans. by Jamie McKendrick
PMC 9780141188362
The Gold-Rimmed Spectacles
trans. by Jamie McKendrick
PMC 9780141192154
The Heron
trans. by Jamie McKendrick
PMC 9780141192147
The Smell of Hay
trans. by Jamie McKendrick
PMC 9780141192123
Within the Walls
trans. by Jamie McKendrick
PMC 9780141192161

BATAILLE, GEORGES
- *Blue of Noon*
    - trans. by Harry Mathews
    - PMC 9780141195544
- *Eroticism*
    - trans. by Mary Dalwood
    - PMC 9780141195568
- *L'Abbé C*
    - trans. by Philip A. Facey
    - PMC 9780141195537
- *Literature and Evil*
    - trans. by Alastair Hamilton
    - PMC 9780141195575
- *My Mother, Madame Edwarda, The Dead Man*
    - trans. by Austryn Wainhouse
    - PMC 9780141195551
- *Story of the Eye*
    - trans. by Joachim Neugroschel
    - PMC 9780141185385

BATES, H. E.
- *Fair Stood the Wind for France*
    - PMC 9780141188164

BAUDELAIRE, CHARLES-PIERRE
- *Selected Poems*
    - trans. by Carol Clark
    - PC 9780140446241

Selected Writings on Art and Literature
    trans. by P. E. Charvet
    PC 9780140446067

BAUM, L. FRANK
The Life and Adventures of Santa Claus
    HB 9780143128533
The Wizard of Oz and Other Wonderful Books of Oz
    HB 9780143138686; Deluxe 9780143106630

BEAUMARCHAIS, PIERRE-AUGUSTIN
The Barber of Seville and *The Marriage of Figaro*
    trans. by John Wood
    PC 9780140441338

BEAUMONT, CHARLES
Perchance to Dream: Selected Stories
    PC 9780143107651

Beauty and the Beast: Classic Tales About Animal Brides and Grooms from Around the World
    ed. by Maria Tatar
    PC 9780143111696

BECKETT, SAMUEL
The End
    PM 9780241338971
First Love and Other Novellas
    PMC 9780141180151

BECKFORD, WILLIAM
Vathek and Other Stories
PC 9780140435306
see also *Three Gothic Novels*

BEDE
Ecclesiastical History of the English People
trans. by Leo Sherley-Price, R. E. Latham &
D. H. Farmer
PC 9780140445657

BEGLEY, LOUIS
Wartime Lies
PMC 9780141188690

BEHN, APHRA
Oroonoko
PC 9780140439885
Oroonoko, The Rover and Other Works
PC 9780140433388

BELL, GERTRUDE
A Woman in Arabia: The Writings of the Queen of the Desert
PC 9780143107378

BELLOW, SAUL
The Actual
PMC 9780141188843

The Adventures of Augie March
 PMC 9780141184869
Collected Stories
 PMC 9780141188782
Dangling Man
 PMC 9780141188775
The Dean's December
 PMC 9780141188867
Henderson the Rain King
 PMC 9780141188805
Herzog
 PMC 9780141184876
Humboldt's Gift
 PMC 9780141188768
It All Adds Up
 PMC 9780241401989
More Die of Heartbreak
 PMC 9780141188799
Mr Sammler's Planet
 PMC 9780141188812
Ravelstein
 PMC 9780141188850
Seize the Day
 PMC 9780141184852
To Jerusalem and Back
 PMC 9780141188874

The Victim
    PMC 9780141188836

BELY, ANDREI
Petersburg
    trans. by David McDuff
    PC 9780141191744

BENEDETTI, MARIO
Springtime in a Broken Mirror
    trans. by Nick Caistor
    PMC 9780241302620
The Truce
    trans. by Harry Morales
    PMC 9780141396859
Who Among Us?
    trans. by Nick Caistor
    PMC 9780241350997

BENEDICT
The Rule of Benedict
    trans. by Caroline White
    PC 9780140449969

BENJAMIN, WALTER
One-Way Street and Other Writings
    trans. by J. A. Underwood
    PMC 9780141189475

Unpacking My Library
    trans. by J. A. Underwood
    Archive 9780241747261
The Work of Art in the Age of Mechanical Reproduction
    trans. by J. A. Underwood
    Great Ideas 9780141036199

BENNETT, ARNOLD
Anna of the Five Towns
    PMC 9780241255773
The Card
    PMC 9780241255544
The Old Wives' Tale
    PC 9780141442112
Riceyman Steps
    PMC 9780241255797

BENSON, E. F.
Mapp and Lucia
    PMC 9780141187686

BENTHAM, JEREMY
Utilitarianism and Other Essays
    PC 9780140432725

Beowulf
> ed. by Michael Alexander (*A Glossed Text*)
> PC 9780140433777
> trans. by Michael Alexander
> PC 9780140449310

BERGER, JOHN
The Red Tenda of Bologna
> PM 9780241339015

Steps Towards a Small Theory of the Visible
> Great Ideas 9780241472873

Understanding a Photograph
> Design 9780141392028

Ways of Seeing
> Design 9780141035796

Why Look at Animals?
> Great Ideas 9780141043975

BERKELEY, GEORGE
Principles of Human Knowledge and *Three Dialogues*
> PC 9780140432930

BERLIN, ISAIAH
Russian Thinkers
> PC 9780141442204

BERNANOS, GEORGES
Diary of a Country Priest
trans. by Howard Curtis
PC 9780241381809

BERNHARD, THOMAS
Old Masters: A Comedy
trans. by Ewald Osers
PMC 9780241459423

BEROUL
The Romance of Tristan
trans. by Alan S. Fedrick
PC 9780140442304

BERRY, WENDELL
What I Stand for Is What I Stand On
Green 9780241514658
Why I Am Not Going to Buy a Computer
PM 9780241337561

The Bhagavad Gita
trans. by Laurie L. Patton
PC 9780140447903

The Bible
ed. by David Norton
PC 9780141441511

BIERCE, AMBROSE
The Enlarged Devil's Dictionary
PMC 9780141185927

BLACKMORE, R. D.
Lorna Doone
PC 9780143039327

BLAKE, WILLIAM
The Complete Poems
PC 9780140422153
Selected Poems
PC 9780140424461
Songs of Innocence and of Experience
Clothbound Poetry 9780241303054
Tyger, Tyger
LBC 9780241251966

BLIXEN, KAREN
(Isak Dinesen)
The Angelic Avengers
PMC 9780141186436
Babette's Feast
LCC 9780241597286
Babette's Feast and Other Stories
PMC 9780141393766
The Dreaming Child
Archive 9780241746950

Out of Africa
    PMC 9780141183336
Seven Gothic Tales
    PMC 9780141187198
Shadows on the Grass
    PMC 9780140180435
Winter's Tales
    PMC 9780141185880

BLUNDEN, EDMUND
Undertones of War
    PMC 9780141184364

BLY, NELLIE
Around the World in Seventy-Two Days and Other Writings
    PC 9780143107408

BLYTHE, RONALD
Akenfield
    PMC 9780141187921

BOCCACCIO, GIOVANNI
The Decameron
    trans. by G. H. McWilliam
    PC 9780140449303
Tales from the Decameron
    trans. by Peter Hainsworth
    PC 9780141191331

BOETHIUS
   The Consolation of Philosophy
      trans. by Victor Watts
      PC 9780140447804

BONATTI, WALTER
   The Mountains of My Life
      trans. by Robert Marshall
      PMC 9780141192918

The Book of Common Prayer
      ed. by James Wood
      Deluxe 9780143106562

The Book of Dede Korkut
      trans. by Geoffrey Lewis
      PC 9780141199030

The Book of Magic from Antiquity to the Enlightenment
      ed. by Brian Copenhaver
      PC 9780141393148

The Book of Taliesin: Poems of Warfare and Praise in an Enchanted Britain
      trans. by Gwyneth Lewis & Rowan Williams
      PC 9780141396934

BORGES, JORGE LUIS

The Aleph
trans. by Andrew Hurley
PMC 9780141183831

The Book of Sand and *Shakespeare's Memory*
trans. by Andrew Hurley
PMC 9780141183824

Brodie's Report
trans. by Andrew Hurley
PMC 9780141183862

Fictions
trans. by Andrew Hurley
PMC 9780141183848

The Garden of Forking Paths
trans. by Donald A. Yates, Andrew Hurley & James E. Irby
PM 9780241339053

Labyrinths
ed. by Donald A. Yates & James E. Irby
PMC 9780141184845

The Library of Babel
trans. by Andrew Hurley
LCC 9780241630860

The Perpetual Race of Achilles and the Tortoise
trans. by Esther Allen, Suzanne Jill Levine & Eliot Weinberger
Great Ideas 9780141192949

Selected Poems
    ed. by Alexander Coleman
    PMC 9780141181110
The Total Library: Non-Fiction 1922–1986
    trans. by Esther Allen, Suzanne Jill Levine & Eliot Weinberger
    PMC 9780141183022
A Universal History of Iniquity
    trans. by Andrew Hurley
    PMC 9780141183855

BOROWSKI, TADEUSZ
This Way for the Gas, Ladies and Gentlemen
    trans. by Barbara Vedder
    PC 9780140186246

BOSWELL, JAMES
The Journal of a Tour to the Hebrides
in *A Journey to the Western Islands of Scotland* and *The Journal of a Tour to the Hebrides*
    (see also Samuel Johnson)
    PC 9780140432213
The Life of Samuel Johnson
    PC 9780140436624
London Journal 1762–1763
    PC 9780140436501

BOWLES, PAUL
Collected Stories
PMC 9780141191355
Let It Come Down
PMC 9780141182209
The Sheltering Sky
PMC 9780141187778
The Spider's House
PMC 9780141191362
Up Above the World
PMC 9780141191386

BOYE, KARIN
Kallocain
trans. by David McDuff
PC 9780241608302

BRADDON, MARY ELIZABETH
Lady Audley's Secret
PC 9780140435849; PEL 9780141198842

BRADLEY, A. C.
Shakespearean Tragedy
PC 9780140530193

BRANCATI, VITALIANO
Beautiful Antonio
trans. by Patrick Creagh
PMC 9780141189062

BRAND, DIONNE
Nomenclature: New and Collected Poems
PMC 9780241639795

BRECHT, BERTOLT
The Caucasian Chalk Circle
trans. by Eric Bentley
PMC 9780141189161
The Good Woman of Setzuan
trans. by Eric Bentley
PMC 9780141189178

BRENAN, GERALD
South from Granada
PMC 9780141189321

BRETON, ANDRÉ
Nadja
trans. by Richard Howard
PMC 9780141180892

BRILLAT-SAVARIN, JEAN-ANTHELME
The Physiology of Taste
trans. by Anne Drayton
PC 9780140446142

BRODSKY, JOSEPH
Less Than One: Selected Essays
PMC 9780141196510

On Grief and Reason: Essays
  PMC 9780241952719
Selected Poems 1968–1996
  ed. by Ann Kjellberg
  PMC 9780241464823
Watermark: An Essay on Venice
  PMC 9780141391496

BRONTË, ANNE
Agnes Grey
  PC 9780140432107
The Tenant of Wildfell Hall
  PC 9780140434743; Clothbound 9780241198957;
  PEL 9780141199351

BRONTË, CHARLOTTE
Jane Eyre
  PC 9780141441146; Clothbound 9780141040387;
  PEL 9780141198859; Deluxe 9780143106159
The Professor
  PC 9780140433111
Shirley
  PC 9780141439860
Tales of Angria
  PC 9780140435092
Villette
  PC 9780140434798; Clothbound 9780241198964;
  PEL 9780141199887

BRONTË, EMILY
The Complete Poems
PC 9780140423525
The Night is Darkening Round Me
LBC 9780141398471
No Coward Soul Is Mine
Archive 9780241746769
Wuthering Heights
PC 9780141439556; Clothbound 9780141040356;
PEL 9780141199085; Deluxe 9780143105435

BROOK, PETER
The Empty Space
PMC 9780141189222

BROWN, ELAINE
A Taste of Power: A Black Woman's Story
PMC 9780241537343

BROWNE, SIR THOMAS
The Major Works
PC 9780140431094

BROWNING, ELIZABETH BARRETT
Aurora Leigh and Other Poems
PC 9780140434125

BROWNING, ROBERT
Selected Poems
PC 9780140437263

BUCHAN, JOHN
Greenmantle
NS 9780141035840
The Thirty-Nine Steps
PC 9780141441177; PEL 9780241341254;
NS 9780141031262

BÜCHNER, GEORG
Complete Plays, Lenz and Other Writings
trans. by John Reddick
PC 9780140445862

BUCKLER, RICH
with Don McGregor, Billy Graham, Stan Lee &
Jack Kirby
Black Panther
Marvel 9780143135814; Marvel HB 9780143135807

Buddhist Meditation: Classic Teachings from Tibet
trans. by Kurtis R. Schaeffer
PC 9780143111467

Buddhist Scriptures
trans. by Donald S. Lopez, Jr.
PC 9780140447583

BULGAKOV, MIKHAIL
A Dead Man's Memoir (A Theatrical Novel)
trans. by Andrew Bromfield
PC 9780140455144
A Dog's Heart
trans. by Andrew Bromfield
PC 9780140455151; Archive 9780241746288
The Master and Margarita
trans. by Richard Pevear & Larissa Volokhonsky
PC 9780140455465; Clothbound 9780241552674

BULOSAN, CARLOS
America Is in the Heart
PC 9780143134039

BUNIN, IVAN
The Gentleman from San Francisco and Other Stories
trans. by David Richards & Sophie Lund
PMC 9780140185522

BUNYAN, JOHN
Grace Abounding to the Chief of Sinners
PC 9780140432800
The Pilgrim's Progress
PC 9780141439716

BURCKHARDT, JACOB
The Civilization of the Renaissance in Italy
trans. by S. G. C. Middlemore
PC 9780140445343

BURGESS, ANTHONY
A Clockwork Orange
PMC 9780141182605
A Clockwork Orange: Restored Edition
NS 9780141197531
M/F
PMC 9780141187808

BURKE, EDMUND
A Philosophical Enquiry into the Sublime and Beautiful
PC 9780140436259
Reflections on the Revolution in France
PC 9780140432046

BURNETT, FRANCES HODGSON
The Secret Garden
Deluxe 9780143106456

BURNEY, FRANCES
Evelina
PC 9780140433470; PEL 9780141198866
Journals and Letters
PC 9780140436242

BURNS, ROBERT
Selected Poems
PC 9780140423822

BURROUGHS, EDGAR RICE
  Tarzan of the Apes
    NS 9780141036533

BURROUGHS, WILLIAM S.
  And the Hippos Were Boiled in Their Tanks
  with Jack Kerouac
    PMC 9780141189673
  The Cat Inside
    PMC 9780141189901
  Cities of the Red Night
    PMC 9780141189932
  Exterminator!
    PMC 9780141189840
  The Finger
    PM 9780241339077
  Interzone
    PMC 9780141189871
  The Job: Interviews with William S. Burroughs
  with Daniel Odier
    PMC 9780141189857
  Junky
    PMC 9780141189826
  Letters 1945–1959
    PMC 9780141189888
  My Education
    PMC 9780141189895

Naked Lunch
   PMC 9780141189765; Clothbound 9780241284636
Nova Express
   PMC 9780141396064
The Place of Dead Roads
   PMC 9780141189796
Queer
   PMC 9780141189918
Rub Out the Words: Letters 1959–1974
   PMC 9780141189802
The Soft Machine
   PMC 9780141189789
The Ticket That Exploded
   PMC 9780141189772
The Western Lands
   PMC 9780141189949
The Wild Boys
   PMC 9780141189833
The Yage Letters
with Allen Ginsberg
   PMC 9780141189864

JOHN & SAL BUSCEMA
   with Stan Lee, Jack Kirby, Roy Thomas & Don Heck
   The Avengers
      Marvel 9780143135791; Marvel HB 9780143135784

BURTON, ROBERT
The Anatomy of Melancholy
PC 9780141192284

BUTLER, SAMUEL
Erewhon
PC 9780140430578
The Way of All Flesh
PC 9780140430127

BYRON, GEORGE GORDON LORD
Don Juan
PC 9780140424522
Selected Poems
PC 9780140424508

BYRON, ROBERT
The Road to Oxiana
PC 9780141442099

C

CAESAR, JULIUS
The Civil War
trans. by Jane F. Gardner
PC 9780140441871
The Conquest of Gaul
trans. by S. A. Handford, rev. Jane F. Gardner
PC 9780140444339

CAICEDO, ANDRÉS
Liveforever
trans. by Frank Wynne
PMC 9780141196688

CALASSO, ROBERTO
K.
trans. by Geoffrey Brock
PMC 9780241399439
Ka
trans. by Tim Parks
PMC 9780241399224

The Marriage of Cadmus and Harmony
    trans. by Tim Parks
    PMC 9780241399200
Tiepolo Pink
    trans. by Alastair McEwen
    PMC 9780241399422

CALVINO, ITALO
  Collection of Sand
    trans. by Martin McLaughlin
    PMC 9780141193748
  The Complete Cosmicomics
    trans. by Martin McLaughlin, Tim Parks &
    William Weaver
    PMC 9780141189680
  Cosmicomics
    trans. by Martin McLaughlin, Tim Parks &
    William Weaver
    LCC 9780241573709
  The Distance of the Moon
    trans. by Martin McLaughlin, Tim Parks &
    William Weaver
    PM 9780241339107
  Fantastic Tales
    ed. by Italo Calvino
    PMC 9780141190129

Hermit in Paris
   trans. by Martin McLaughlin
   PMC 9780141189758
Into the War
   trans. by Martin McLaughlin
   PMC 9780141193731
Italian Folktales
   trans. by George Martin
   PMC 9780141181349
Letters 1941–1985
   trans. by Martin McLaughlin
   PMC 9780141198323
The Narrative of Trajan's Column
   trans. by Martin McLaughlin
   Great Ideas 9780241472859
Numbers in the Dark
   trans. by Tim Parks
   PMC 9780141189741
The Path to the Spiders' Nests
   trans. by Archibald Colquhoun, rev. Martin McLaughlin
   PMC 9780141189734
The Road to San Giovanni
   trans. by Tim Parks
   PMC 9780141189710

Six Memos for the Next Millennium
    trans. by Geoffrey Brock
    PMC 9780241275955
Under the Jaguar Sun
    trans. by William Weaver
    PMC 9780141189727; Archive 9780241752371
Why Read the Classics?
    trans. by Martin McLaughlin
    PMC 9780141189703
The Written World and the Unwritten World: Collected Non-Fiction
    trans. by Ann Goldstein
    PMC 9780141394923

CAMÕES, LUIS VAZ DE
The Lusiads
    trans. by William Atkinson
    PC 9780140440263

CAMUS, ALBERT
Caligula and Three Other Plays
    (*Caligula*, *The Misunderstanding*, *State of Emergency*, *The Just*)
    trans. by Ryan Bloom
    PMC 9780241657799
Committed Writings
    trans. by Justin O'Brien & Sandra Smith
    PMC 9780241400401

Create Dangerously
    trans. by Justin O'Brien
    PM 9780241339121

Exile and the Kingdom: Stories
    trans. by Carol Cosman
    PMC 9780141188256

The Fall
    trans. by Robin Buss
    PMC 9780141187945; LCC 9780241630778;
    NS 9780241458884

The Fastidious Assassins
    trans. by Anthony Bower
    Great Ideas 9780141036625

The First Man
    trans. by David Hapgood
    PMC 9780141185231

A Happy Death
    trans. by Richard Howard
    PMC 9780141186580

The Myth of Sisyphus
    trans. by Justin O'Brien
    PMC 9780141182001; Great Ideas 9780141023991

The Outsider
    trans. by Sandra Smith
    PMC 9780141198064; Clothbound 9780241554401;
    NS 9780241458853

The Outsider: Manga Edition
 illus. by Ryota Kurumado; trans. by Ros Schwartz
 PMC 9780241703731
Personal Writings
 trans. by Ellen Conroy Kennedy & Justin O'Brien
 PMC 9780241400272
The Plague
 trans. by Robin Buss
 PMC 9780141185132; NS 9780241458877
The Rebel
 trans. by Anthony Bower
 PMC 9780141182018
Reflections on the Guillotine
 trans. by Justin O'Brien
 Great Ideas 9780241475225
A Short Guide to Towns Without a Past
 trans. by Ellen Conroy Kennedy & Justin O'Brien
 Archive 9780241752012
Speaking Out: Lectures and Speeches 1937–58
 trans. by Quintin Hoare
 PMC 9780241400364

CANETTI, ELIAS
Kafka's Other Trial
 trans. by Christopher Middleton
 PMC 9780141195636

The Voices of Marrakesh: A Record of a Visit
trans. by J. A. Underwood
PMC 9780141195629

CAO XUEQIN
The Story of the Stone
Volume 1: The Golden Days
trans. by David Hawkes
PC 9780140442939
Volume 2: The Crab-Flower Club
trans. by David Hawkes
PC 9780140443264
Volume 3: The Warning Voice
trans. by David Hawkes
PC 9780140443707
Volume 4: The Debt of Tears
with Gao E
trans. by John Minford
PC 9780140443714
Volume 5: The Dreamer Wakes
with Gao E
trans. by John Minford
PC 9780140443721

ČAPEK, KAREL
War with the Newts
trans. by M. & R. Weatherall
PMC 9780241343456

CAPETILLO, LUISA
A Nation of Women
trans. by Alan West-Durán
PC 9780143136071

CAPOTE, TRUMAN
Answered Prayers
PMC 9780141185934
Breakfast at Tiffany's
PMC 9780141182797; LCC 9780241597262
A Capote Reader
PMC 9780141185309
A Christmas Memory
PMC 9780241474426
The Complete Stories
PMC 9780141188089
The Duke in His Domain
PM 9780241339145
The Early Stories of Truman Capote
PMC 9780241202425
In Cold Blood
PMC 9780141182575
Music for Chameleons
PMC 9780141184616
Other Voices, Other Rooms
PMC 9780141187655

Summer Crossing
 PMC 9780141188584

CARLYLE, THOMAS
Selected Writings
 PC 9780141396767

CARPENTER, DON
Hard Rain Falling
 PMC 9780241766934

CARPENTIER, ALEJO
Explosion in a Cathedral
 trans. by Adrian Nathan West
 PC 9780143133889
The Lost Steps
 trans. by Adrian Nathan West
 PC 9780143133896

CARR, E. H.
What is History?
 PMC 9780141010205

CARR, J. L.
How Steeple Sinderby Wanderers Won the F.A. Cup
 PMC 9780241252345
A Month in the Country
 PMC 9780141182308

CARRINGTON, DOROTHY
Granite Island: Portrait of Corsica
PC 9780141442273

CARRINGTON, LEONORA
The Hearing Trumpet
PMC 9780141187990
The Skeleton's Holiday
PM 9780241339169

CARROLL, LEWIS
Alice's Adventures in Wonderland and Through the Looking Glass
PC 9780141439761; Clothbound 9780141192468;
PEL 9780141199689; Deluxe 9780143107620
with artwork by Yayoi Kusama
HB 9780141197302
The Hunting of the Snark
PC 9780140434910
Jabberwocky and Other Nonsense: Collected Poems
PC 9780141192789; Clothbound 9780141195940

CARSON, RACHEL
Man's War Against Nature
Green 9780241514450
Silent Spring
PMC 9780141184944

CĂRTĂRESCU, MIRCEA
Nostalgia
    trans. by Julian Semilian
    PMC 9780241448915

CARTER, ANGELA
The Fairy Tales of Charles Perrault
    PMC 9780141189956
Heroes and Villains
    PMC 9780141192383
The Infernal Desire Machines of Doctor Hoffman
    PMC 9780141192390

CASANOVA, GIACOMO
The Story of My Life
    trans. by Stephen Sartarelli & Sophie Hawkes
    PC 9780140439151

CASTIGLIONE, BALDESAR
The Book of the Courtier
    trans. by George Bull
    PC 9780140441925

CATHER, WILLA
Death Comes for the Archbishop
    PMC 9780241338261
A Lost Lady
    Archive 9780241752050

My Ántonia
   PMC 9780241338322
O Pioneers!
   PMC 9780241338353
The Song of the Lark
   PMC 9780241338162

CATULLUS
  I Hate and I Love
    trans. by Peter Whigham
    LBC 9780141398594
  The Poems
    trans. by Peter Whigham
    PC 9780140449815

CAVAFY, C. P.
  Selected Poems
    trans. by Avi Sharon
    PC 9780141185613

CAVENDISH, MARGARET
  The Blazing World
   Archive 9780241746813
  The Blazing World and Other Writings
   PC 9780140433722

CELAN, PAUL
Selected Poems
trans. by Michael Hamburger
PMC 9780140189209

CELLINI, BENVENUTO
The Autobiography of Benvenuto Cellini
trans. by George Bull
PC 9780140447187

A Celtic Miscellany
trans. by Kenneth Hurlstone Jackson
PC 9780141398853

CERVANTES, MIGUEL
Don Quixote
trans. by John Rutherford
PC 9780140449099; Clothbound 9780241347768
Exemplary Stories
trans. by C. A. Jones
PC 9780140442489

CÉSAIRE, AIMÉ
Return to My Native Land
trans. by John Berger & Anna Bostock
PMC 9780241535394

CHAGALL, MARC
  My Life
    trans. by Dorothy Williams
    PMC 9780241331415

CHANDLER, RAYMOND
  The Big Sleep and *Farewell, My Lovely*
    Crime 9780241654149
  The Big Sleep and Other Novels
    (*The Big Sleep*, *Farewell, My Lovely*, *The Long Goodbye*)
    PMC 9780141182612
  The Lady in the Lake and Other Novels
    (*The Lady in the Lake*, *The High Window*, *The Little Sister*)
    PMC 9780141186085

CHANG, EILEEN
  Half a Lifelong Romance
    trans. by Karen S. Kingsbury & Eileen Chang
    PMC 9780141189390
  Jasmine Tea
    trans. by Eileen Chang, Karen S. Kingsbury &
    Eva Hung
    Archive 9780241752302
  Love in a Fallen City
    trans. by Karen S. Kingsbury & Eileen Chang
    PMC 9780141189369

Lust, Caution
    trans. by Julia Lovell, Karen S. Kingsbury, Janet Ng, Simon Patton & Eva Hung
    PMC 9780141034386

CHAPLIN, CHARLES
My Autobiography
    PMC 9780141011479

CHASE, OWEN
with Thomas Nickerson & others
The Loss of the Ship Essex *Sunk by a Whale: First-Person Accounts*
    PC 9780140437966

CHATEAUBRIAND, FRANÇOIS-RENÉ DE
Memoirs from Beyond the Tomb
    trans. by Robert Baldick
    PC 9780141393124

CHAUCER, GEOFFREY
The Canterbury Tales
    trans. by Nevill Coghill
    PC 9780140424386; Clothbound 9780141393216
    ed. by Jill Mann
    PC 9780140422344
    retold by Peter Ackroyd
    PC 9780141442297

The Canterbury Tales: The First Fragment
    ed. by Michael Alexander
    PC 9780140434095
The Canterbury Tales: A Selection
    trans. by Colin Wilcockson
    PC 9780140424454
Love Visions
    trans. by Brian Stone
    PC 9780140444087
Troilus and Criseyde
    trans. by Nevill Coghill
    PC 9780140442397
    ed. by Barry Windeatt
    PC 9780140424218

CHEKHOV, ANTON
About Love
    trans. by Ronald Wilks
    LCC 9780241619766
Fifty-Two Stories
    trans. by Richard Pevear & Larissa Volokhonsky
    PC 9780241444245
Gooseberries
    trans. by Ronald Wilks
    LBC 9780141397092

The Lady with the Little Dog and Other Stories, 1896–1904
   trans. by Ronald Wilks
   PC 9780140447873

A Life in Letters
   trans. by Rosamund Bartlett & Anthony Phillips
   PC 9780140449228

A Nervous Breakdown
   trans. by Ronald Wilks
   LBC 9780241251782

Plays
   (*Ivanov*, *The Seagull*, *Uncle Vanya*, *Three Sisters*, *The Cherry Orchard*)
   trans. by Peter Carson
   PC 9780140447330

The Shooting Party
   trans. by Ronald Wilks
   PC 9780140448986

The Steppe and Other Stories, 1887–91
   trans. by Ronald Wilks
   PC 9780140447859

Ward No. 6 and Other Stories, 1892–1895
   trans. by Ronald Wilks
   PC 9780140447866

CHESTERTON, G. K.
The Complete Father Brown Stories
   PC 9780141193854

Father Brown: Selected Stories
    PEL 9780241652671
The Man Who Was Thursday
    PC 9780141191461; PEL 9780141199771
The Napoleon of Notting Hill
    PC 9780241698631

CHILDERS, ERSKINE
The Riddle of the Sands
    PC 9780143106326

CHÖGYEL, TENZIN
The Life of the Buddha
    trans. by Kurtis R. Schaeffer
    PC 9780143107200

CHŌMEI, KAMO NO
Hōjōki
in *Essays in Idleness* and *Hōjōki*
    trans. by Meredith McKinney
    (see also Yoshida Kenkō)
    PC 9780141192109

CHOPIN, KATE
The Awakening
    PEL 9780241341421; LCC 9780241630785
The Awakening and Selected Stories
    PC 9780142437322

The Story of an Hour
  Archive 9780241746868

CHRÉTIEN DE TROYES
Arthurian Romances
  trans. by William W. Kibler & Carleton W. Carroll
  PC 9780140445213

CHRISTINE DE PIZAN
The Treasure of the City of Ladies
  trans. by Sarah Lawson
  PC 9780140449501

CHRISTOPHER, JOHN
The Death of Grass
  PMC 9780141190174

CHUANG TZU
The Book of Chuang Tzu
  trans. by Martin Palmer, Elizabeth Breuilly,
  Chang Wai Ming & Jay Ramsay
  PC 9780140455373
The Tao of Nature
  trans. by Martin Palmer, Elizabeth Breuilly &
  Jay Ramsay
  Great Ideas 9780141192741

CHURCHILL, WINSTON
Blood, Toil, Tears and Sweat: Winston Churchill's Famous Speeches
PC 9780141442068
The Second World War
Volume I: The Gathering Storm
NS 9780141441726
Volume II: Their Finest Hour
NS 9780141441733
Volume III: The Grand Alliance
NS 9780141441740
Volume IV: The Hinge of Fate
NS 9780141441757
Volume V: Closing the Ring
NS 9780141441764
Volume VI: Triumph and Tragedy
NS 9780141441771
We Will All Go Down Fighting to the End
Great Ideas 9780141192536
The World Crisis 1911–1918
PC 9780141442051

CICERO
In Defence of the Republic
trans. by Siobhán McElduff
PC 9780140455533

Murder Trials
    trans. by Michael Grant
    PC 9780140442885

The Nature of the Gods
    trans. by Horace C. P. McGregor
    PC 9780140442656

On Government
    trans. by Michael Grant
    PC 9780140445954

On Living and Dying Well
    trans. by Thomas Habinek
    PC 9780140455564

On the Good Life
    trans. by Michael Grant
    PC 9780140442441

Selected Letters
    trans. by D. R. Shackleton Bailey
    PC 9780140444582

Selected Political Speeches
    trans. by Michael Grant
    PC 9780140442144

Selected Works
    trans. by Michael Grant
    PC 9780140440997

CIORAN, E. M.
> *A Short History of Decay*
>> trans. by Richard Howard
>> PMC 9780241343463
> *The Trouble with Being Born*
>> trans. by Richard Howard
>> PMC 9780241467275

The Cistercian World: Monastic Writings of the Twelfth Century
> trans. by Pauline Matarasso
> PC 9780140433562

CLARE, JOHN
> *Selected Poems*
>> PC 9780140437249

Classical Comedy
> ed. by Erich Segal
> PC 9780140449822

Classical Literary Criticism
> trans. by T. S. Dorsch, rev. Penelope Murray
> PC 9780140446517

CLAUSEWITZ, CARL
> *On War*
>> trans. by J. J. Graham
>> PC 9780140444278

CLELAND, JOHN
    Fanny Hill: Memoirs of a Woman of Pleasure
        PC 9780140432497

CLIFTON, LUCILLE
    Blessing The Boats
        PMC 9780241609019

The Cloud of Unknowing and Other Works
    trans. by A. C. Spearing
        PC 9780140447620

COBB, RICHARD
    French and Germans, Germans and French
        PMC 9780241351314

COBBETT, WILLIAM
    Rural Rides
        PC 9780140435795

COHEN, ALBERT
    Her Lover (Belle du Seigneur)
    trans. by David Coward
        PMC 9780141188300

COLEGATE, ISABEL
    The Shooting Party
        PMC 9780141188676

COLERIDGE, SAMUEL TAYLOR
The Complete Poems
PC 9780140423532
Lyrical Ballads
with William Wordsworth
PC 9780140424621; Clothbound Poetry
9780241303108
Selected Poetry
PC 9780140424294

COLLINS, NORMAN
London Belongs to Me
PMC 9780141442334

COLLINS, WILKIE
Armadale
PC 9780140434118
The Law and the Lady
PC 9780140436075
The Moonstone
PC 9780140434088; PEL 9780141198873
No Name
PC 9780140433975
The Woman in White
PC 9780141439617; Clothbound 9780141192420;
PEL 9780141389431

COLLODI, CARLO
The Adventures of Pinocchio
trans. by John Hooper & Anna Kraczyna
PC 9780143136095

COLUMBUS, CHRISTOPHER
The Four Voyages
PC 9780140442175

Comic Sagas and Tales from Iceland
ed. by Viðar Hreinsson
PC 9780140447743

The Complete Dead Sea Scrolls in English
trans. by Geza Vermes
PC 9780141197319

Con Men and Cutpurses: Scenes from the Hogarthian Underworld
ed. by Lucy Moore
PC 9780140437607

CONDÉ, MARYSE
Crossing the Mangrove
trans. by Richard Philcox
PMC 9780241530054
Segu
trans. by Barbara Bray
PMC 9780241293515

Tales from the Heart
    trans. by Richard Philcox
    Archive 9780241752432

CONFUCIUS
The Analects
    trans. by D. C. Lau
    PC 9780140443486
    trans. by Annping Chin
    PC 9780143106852
The First Ten Books
    trans. by D. C. Lau
    Great Ideas 9780141023809
The Most Venerable Book (Shang Shu)
    trans. by Martin Palmer, Jay Ramsay & Victoria Finlay
    PC 9780141197463

CONGREVE, WILLIAM
The Way of the World and Other Plays
    PC 9780141441856
see also *Three Restoration Comedies*

CONNELL, EVAN S.
Mr Bridge
    PMC 9780141198668
Mrs Bridge
    PMC 9780141198651

CONRAD, JOSEPH
- *Heart of Darkness*
  PC 9780141441672; Clothbound 9780241655573;
  PEL 9780141199788; Deluxe 9780143106586
- *The Lagoon*
  LCC 9780241619773
- *Lord Jim*
  PC 9780141441610
- *Nostromo*
  PC 9780141441634
- *The Secret Agent*
  PC 9780141441580; PEL 9780141199559
- *The Shadow-Line*
  PMC 9780140180978
- *Typhoon and Other Stories*
  PC 9780141441955
- *Under Western Eyes*
  PC 9780141441948
- *Victory*
  PC 9780241189658

CONSTANT, BENJAMIN
- *Adolphe*
  PC 9780140441345

The Constitution of the United States
  LBC 9780241318492

COOK, JAMES
> *The Journals of Captain Cook*
> PC 9780140436471

COOKE, ALISTAIR
> *Letter from America 1946–2004*
> PMC 9780241513361

COOPER, ANNA JULIA
> *The Portable Anna Julia Cooper*
> PC 9780143135067

COOPER, DUFF
> *Operation Heartbreak*
> PC 9780241799918

COOPER, JAMES FENIMORE
> *The Last of the Mohicans*
> PC 9780140390247

COOVER, ROBERT
> *Briar Rose* and *Spanking the Maid*
> PMC 9780141192994
> *Gerald's Party*
> PMC 9780141192987
> *Pricksongs & Descants*
> PMC 9780141192956

CORNEILLE, PIERRE
The Cid, Cinna, The Theatrical Illusion
trans. by John Cairncross
PC 9780140443127
see also *Four French Plays*

CORVO (FR. ROLFE), FREDERICK BARON
Hadrian the Seventh
PC 9780241313022

CRABBE, GEORGE
Selected Poems
PC 9780141396255

CRANE, STEPHEN
Maggie: A Girl of the Streets and Other Tales of New York
PC 9780140437973
The Red Badge of Courage and Other Stories
PC 9780143039358

CREWS, HARRY
A Childhood: The Biography of a Place
PC 9780143135333
The Gospel Singer
PC 9780143135098
The Knockout Artist
PC 9780143137931

CULLINAN, THOMAS
The Beguiled
PMC 9780241321812

CURTIUS RUFUS, QUINTUS
The History of Alexander
trans. by John Yardley
PC 9780140444124

CUSTINE, ASTOLPHE DE
Letters from Russia
trans. by Robin Buss
PC 9780141394510

The Cynic Philosophers from Diogenes to Julian
trans. by Robert Dobbin
PC 9780141192222

D

DAHL, ROALD
Charlie and the Chocolate Factory
PMC 9780141394589; Deluxe 9780143106333
James and the Giant Peach
Deluxe 9780143106340
Lamb to the Slaughter
Archive 9780241747018
Over to You: Ten Stories of Flyers and Flying
PMC 9780141189659
Someone Like You
PMC 9780141189642
Ten Short Stories
Student 9780140817799

DAI QING
The Most Dammed Country in the World
Green 9780241514597

DAMPIER, WILLIAM
A New Voyage Round the World
PC 9780241413289

DANTE

Circles of Hell
trans. by Robin Kirkpatrick
LBC 9780141980225

Dante in English
ed. by Eric Griffiths & Matthew Reynolds
PC 9780140423884

The Divine Comedy: Inferno, Purgatorio, Paradiso
trans. by Robin Kirkpatrick
PC 9780141197494

Inferno
trans. by Dorothy L. Sayers (as *Hell*)
PC 9780140440065; Archive 9780241752159
trans. by Mark Musa
PC 9780142437223
trans. by Robin Kirkpatrick
PC 9780140448955; Clothbound 9780141195872;
NS 9780141393544

Purgatorio
trans. by Dorothy L. Sayers (as *Purgatory*)
PC 9780140440461
trans. by Mark Musa (as *Purgatory*)
PC 9780140444421
trans. by Robin Kirkpatrick
PC 9780140448962

Paradiso
    trans. by Dorothy L. Sayers & Barbara Reynolds (as *Paradise*)
    PC 9780140441055
    trans. by Mark Musa (as *Paradise*)
    PC 9780140444438
    trans. by Robin Kirkpatrick
    PC 9780140448979
Love That Moves the Sun and Other Stars
    trans. by Robin Kirkpatrick
    LBC 9780241250426
Vita Nuova
    trans. by Barbara Reynolds
    PC 9780140449471
Vita Nuova: A Dual-Language Edition with Parallel Text
    trans. by Virginia Jewiss
    PC 9780143106203

DARMA, BUDI
People from Bloomington
    trans. by Tiffany Tsao
    PC 9780143136606

DARWIN, CHARLES
Autobiographies
    PC 9780140433906

The Descent of Man
  PC 9780140436310
The Expression of the Emotions in Man and Animals
  PC 9780141439440
On Natural Selection
  Great Ideas 9780141018966
On the Origin of Species
  PC 9780140439120
The Voyage of the Beagle
  PC 9780140432688

DAUDET, ALPHONSE
Letters from My Windmill
  trans. by Frederick Davies
  PC 9780140443349

DAVIS, ANGELA Y.
Women, Race & Class
  PMC 9780241408407

The Dawn of Modern Cosmology from Copernicus to Newton
  ed. by Aviva Rothman
  PC 9780241360637

DE BEAUVOIR, SIMONE
The Blood of Others
  trans. by Yvonne Moyse & Roger Senhouse
  PMC 9780241696453

Memoirs of a Dutiful Daughter
    trans. by James Kirkup
    PMC 9780141185330
The Prime of Life
    trans. by Peter Green
    PMC 9780241705391
What Is Existentialism?
    trans. by Marybeth Timmermann
    Great Ideas 9780241475232

DE MONFREID, HENRY
Hashish: A Smuggler's Tale
    trans. by Helen Buchanan Bell
    PC 9780141442105

DE QUINCEY, THOMAS
Confessions of an English Opium-Eater and Other Writings
    PC 9780140439014

DE SADE, THE MARQUIS
The 120 Days of Sodom
    trans. by Will McMorran & Thomas Wynn
    PC 9780141394343
Philosophy in the Boudoir
    trans. by Joachim Neugroschel
    Deluxe 9780143039013

DE SÉVIGNÉ, MADAME
Selected Letters
trans. by Leonard Tancock
PC 9780140444056

The Death of King Arthur
trans. by James Cable
PC 9780140442557

Decadent Poetry from Wilde to Naidu
ed. by Lisa Rodensky
PC 9780140424133

DEFOE, DANIEL
A Journal of the Plague Year
PC 9780140437850
Moll Flanders
PC 9780140433135
Robinson Crusoe
PC 9780141439822; Clothbound 9780141393407;
PEL 9780141199061
Roxana
PC 9780140431490
The Storm
PC 9780141439921
A Tour Through the Whole Island of Great Britain
PC 9780140430660

DEIGHTON, LEN

Berlin Game
PMC 9780241505144
Billion-Dollar Brain
PMC 9780241505168
Blitzkrieg: From the Rise of Hitler to the Fall of Dunkirk
PMC 9780241505212
Blood, Tears and Folly: An Objective Look at World War Two
PMC 9780241505236
Bomber
PMC 9780241493700
Charity
PMC 9780241505250
City of Gold
PMC 9780241505311
Close-Up
PMC 9780241505328
Declarations of War
PMC 9780241505335
An Expensive Place to Die
PMC 9780241505342
Faith
PMC 9780241505366
Fighter: The True Story of the Battle of Britain
PMC 9780241505373
Funeral in Berlin
PMC 9780241505380

Goodbye Mickey Mouse
   PMC 9780241505397
Hope
   PMC 9780241505403
Horse Under Water
   PMC 9780241505410
The IPCRESS File
   PMC 9780241505427
London Match
   PMC 9780241505434
MAMista
   PMC 9780241505441
Mexico Set
   PMC 9780241505458
Only When I Larf
   PMC 9780241505465
Spy Hook
   PMC 9780241505472
Spy Line
   PMC 9780241505489
Spy Sinker
   PMC 9780241505496
Spy Story
   PMC 9780241505519
SS-GB
   PMC 9780241505526; Crime 9780241639238

Twinkle, Twinkle, Little Spy
  PMC 9780241505533
Violent Ward
  PMC 9780241505540
Winter
  PMC 9780241505557
XPD
  PMC 9780241505564
Yesterday's Spy
  PMC 9780241505571

DELAFIELD, E. M.
The Diary of a Provincial Lady
  PMC 9780141191812

DELANY, SAMUEL R.
Driftglass
  Sci-Fi 9780241510575

DELILLO, DON
Americana
  PMC 9780141188232
Libra
  PMC 9780141188225

DENNIS, PATRICK
Auntie Mame: An Irreverent Escapade
  PMC 9780141194127

DESCARTES, RENÉ
Discourse on Method and *The Meditations*
   trans. by F. E. Sutcliffe
   PC 9780140442069
Discourse on Method and Related Writings
   trans. by Desmond M. Clarke
   PC 9780140446999
Meditations
   trans. by Desmond M. Clarke
   Great Ideas 9780141192963
Meditations and Other Metaphysical Writings
   trans. by Desmond M. Clarke
   PC 9780140447019

The Desert Fathers: Sayings of the Early Christian Monks
   trans. by Benedicta Ward
   PC 9780140447316

The Dhammapada
   trans. by Juan Mascaró
   PC 9780140442847; LBC 9780141398815
   trans. by Valerie J. Roebuck
   PC 9780140449419

DIAMOND, JARED
The Last Tree on Easter Island
   Green 9780141997063

DIAZ DEL CASTILLO, BERNAL
The Conquest of New Spain
trans. by J. M. Cohen
PC 9780140441239

DICK, PHILIP K.
The Man in the High Castle
PMC 9780141186672

DICKENS, CHARLES
American Notes
PC 9780140436495
Barnaby Rudge
PC 9780140437287
Bleak House
PC 9780141439723; Clothbound 9780141198354
The Chimes
Archive 9780241746776
A Christmas Carol
HB 9780143122494; PEL 9780141389479
A Christmas Carol and Other Christmas Writings
PC 9780140439052; Clothbound 9780141195858
David Copperfield
PC 9780140439441; Clothbound 9780141394640;
PEL 9780141199160
Dombey and Son
PC 9780140435467

Great Expectations
  PC 9780141439563; Clothbound 9780141040363;
  PEL 9780141198897; Deluxe 9780143106272
Hard Times
  PC 9780141439679; Clothbound 9780141198347;
  PEL 9780141199566
Little Dorrit
  PC 9780141439969
Martin Chuzzlewit
  PC 9780140436143
The Mystery of Edwin Drood
  PC 9780140439267
Nicholas Nickleby
  PC 9780140435122
Night Walks
  Great Ideas 9780141047508
The Old Curiosity Shop
  PC 9780140437423
Oliver Twist
  PC 9780141439747; Clothbound 9780141192499;
  PEL 9780141198880
Our Mutual Friend
  PC 9780140434972
The Pickwick Papers
  PC 9780140436112
Pictures from Italy
  PC 9780140434316

Selected Journalism 1850–1870
   PC 9780140435801
Selected Short Fiction
   PC 9780140431032
Sketches by Boz
   PC 9780140433456
A Tale of Two Cities
   PC 9780141439600; Clothbound 9780141196909;
   PEL 9780141199702
To Be Read at Dusk
   LBC 9780241251584

DICKINSON, EMILY
My Life Had Stood a Loaded Gun
   LBC 9780241251409

DIDEROT, DENIS
Jacques the Fatalist
   trans. by Michael Henry
   PC 9780140444728
The Nun
   trans. by Leonard Tancock
   PC 9780140443004
Rameau's Nephew and *D'Alembert's Dream*
   trans. by Leonard Tancock
   PC 9780140441734

DINESEN, ISAK
   see Karen Blixen

DIO, CASSIUS
The Roman History: The Reign of Augustus
   trans. by Ian Scott-Kilvert
   PC 9780140444483

DITKO, STEVE
   with Stan Lee
The Amazing Spider-Man
   Marvel 9780143135739

DITLEVSEN, TOVE
Childhood, Youth, Dependency: The Copenhagen Trilogy
   trans. by Tiina Nunnally & Michael Favala Goldman
   PMC 9780241457573
The Faces
   trans. by Tiina Nunnally
   PMC 9780241391914
There Lives a Young Girl in Me Who Will Not Die
   trans. by Sophia Hersi Smith & Jennifer Russell
   NS 9780241637364
The Trouble with Happiness and Other Stories
   trans. by Michael Favala Goldman
   PMC 9780241537381

The Umbrella
    trans. by Michael Favala Goldman
    Archive 9780241752258
Vilhelm's Room
    trans. by Sophia Hersi Smith & Jennifer Russell
    Demy 9780241628980

DJILAS, MILOVAN
Conversations with Stalin
    trans. by Michael B. Petrovich
    PMC 9780141393094

DÖBLIN, ALFRED
Berlin Alexanderplatz
    trans. by Michael Hofmann
    PMC 9780141191621

DOCTOROW, E. L.
Billy Bathgate
    PMC 9780241256428
The Book of Daniel
    PMC 9780141188188
Ragtime
    PMC 9780141188171

Domesday Book: A Complete Translation
    ed. by Ann Williams & G. H. Martin
    PC 9780141439945

DONNE, JOHN
Collected Poetry
PC 9780141191577
The Complete English Poems
PC 9780140422092
Selected Poems
PC 9780140424409
Selected Prose
PC 9780141396712

DOS PASSOS, JOHN
Manhattan Transfer
PMC 9780141184487
U.S.A.
(*The 42nd Parallel*, *Nineteen Nineteen*, *The Big Money*)
PMC 9780141185811

DOSTOYEVSKY, FYODOR
The Brothers Karamazov
trans. by David McDuff
PC 9780140449242; Clothbound 9780241655566
Crime and Punishment
trans. by David McDuff
PC 9780140449136; Clothbound 9780241347683
trans. by Oliver Ready
NS 9780141192802

Demons
    trans. by Robert A. Maguire
    PC 9780141441412

The Dream of a Ridiculous Man
    trans. by Ronald Meyer
    Archive 9780241746912

The Gambler and Other Stories
    trans. by Ronald Meyer
    PC 9780140455090

The House of the Dead
    trans. by David McDuff
    PC 9780140444568

The Idiot
    trans. by David McDuff
    PC 9780140447927; Clothbound 9780241739822

The Meek One
    trans. by Ronald Meyer
    LBC 9780141397481

Netochka Nezvanova
    trans. by Jane Kentish
    PC 9780140444551

Notes from Underground and *The Double*
    trans. by Ronald Wilks
    PC 9780140455120

Poor Folk and Other Stories
    trans. by David McDuff
    PC 9780140445053

White Nights
    trans. by Ronald Meyer
    LCC 9780241619780; LBC 9780241252086

DOUGLASS, FREDERICK
Narrative of Frederick Douglass
    PC 9780143107309
The Portable Frederick Douglass
    PC 9780143106814

DOYLE, ARTHUR CONAN
The Adventure of the Blue Carbuncle
    LCC 9780241597002
The Adventure of the Engineer's Thumb and Other Cases
    PEL 9780141395500
The Adventure of the Six Napoleons and Other Cases
    PEL 9780141395548
The Adventures of Sherlock Holmes
    Clothbound 9780241347782; NS 9780141034355
The Adventures of Sherlock Holmes and *The Memoirs of Sherlock Holmes*
    PC 9780140437713
The Five Orange Pips and Other Cases
    PEL 9780141199719
The Hound of the Baskervilles
    PC 9780140437867; Clothbound 9780141192437; PEL 9780141199177

Sherlock Holmes: The Novels
   (*A Study in Scarlet, The Sign of Four, The Hound of the Baskervilles, The Valley of Fear*)
   PC 9780143107132
The Sign of Four
   PC 9780140439076; PEL 9780141395487
A Study in Scarlet
   PC 9780140439083; PEL 9780141395524
The Valley of Fear
   PEL 9780141395562

DRABBLE, MARGARET
A Day in the Life of a Smiling Woman: The Collected Stories
   PMC 9780141196435

DREISER, THEODORE
The Financier
   PC 9780143105541
Sister Carrie
   PC 9780140188288

DRUMMOND DE ANDRADE, CARLOS
Multitudinous Heart: Selected Poems
   trans. by Richard Zenith
   PMC 9780141396958

DRYDEN, JOHN
Selected Poems
PC 9780140439144
Virgil's Aeneid
PC 9780140446272

DU MAURIER, DAPHNE
The Breakthrough
PM 9780241339206
Don't Look Now and Other Stories
PMC 9780141188379

DU MAURIER, GEORGE
Trilby
PC 9780140434033

DU, NGUYỄN
The Song of Kiều
trans. by Timothy Allen
PC 9780241360668

DUMAS, ALEXANDRE
The Black Tulip
trans. by Robin Buss
PC 9780140448924
The Count of Monte Cristo
trans. by Robin Buss
PC 9780140449266; Clothbound 9780141392462

The Man in the Iron Mask
    trans. by Joachim Neugroschel
    PC 9780140439243
The Three Musketeers
    trans. by Richard Pevear
    PC 9780141442341
The Women's War
    trans. by Robin Buss
    PC 9780140449778

DUMAS *FILS*, ALEXANDRE
The Lady of the Camellias
    trans. by Liesl Schillinger
    PC 9780143107026

DURKHEIM, ÉMILE
On Suicide
    trans. by Robin Buss
    PC 9780140449679

DURRELL, GERALD
Birds, Beasts, and Relatives
    PMC 9780241762950
The Garden of the Gods
    PMC 9780241762967
My Family and Other Animals
    PMC 9780241762943; Clothbound 9780241767061

DVĀTRIMŚIKĀ, SIMHĀSANA
Thirty-Two Tales of the Throne of Vikramaditya
trans. by A. N. D. Haksar
PC 9780140455175

DWORKIN, ANDREA
Pornography: Men Possessing Women
PMC 9780241735947
Right-Wing Women
PMC 9780241735930
Woman Hating
PMC 9780241735954

E

Early Christian Lives
    trans. by Carolinne White
    PC 9780140435269

Early Christian Writings
    trans. by Maxwell Staniforth, rev. Andrew Louth
    PC 9780140444759

Early Fiction in England from Geoffrey of Monmouth to Chaucer
    ed. by Laura Ashe
    PC 9780141392875

Early Greek Philosophy
    trans. by Jonathan Barnes
    PC 9780140448153

Early Irish Myths and Sagas
    trans. by Jeffrey Gantz
    PC 9780140443974

ECKERMANN, JOHANN PETER
Conversations with Goethe
trans. by Allan Blunden
PC 9780241421673

ECKHART, MEISTER
Selected Writings
trans. by Oliver Davies
PC 9780140433432

EDGEWORTH, MARIA
The Absentee
PC 9780140436457
Castle Rackrent and *Ennui*
PC 9780140433203

Egil's Saga
trans. by Bernard Scudder
PC 9780140447705

The Egyptian Book of the Dead
trans. by E. A. Wallis Budge
PC 9780140455502

EINHARD
with Notker the Stammerer
Two Lives of Charlemagne
trans. by David Ganz
PC 9780140455052

EKWENSI, CYPRIAN
Jagua Nana
PMC 9780241334997

The Elder Edda: A Book of Viking Lore
trans. by Andy Orchard
PC 9780140435856; NS 9780141393728

ELIOT, GEORGE
Adam Bede
PC 9780140436648
Daniel Deronda
PC 9780140434279
Felix Holt: The Radical
PC 9780140434354
Middlemarch
PC 9780141439549; Clothbound 9780141196893;
PEL 9780141199795; Deluxe 9780143107729
The Mill on the Floss
PC 9780141439624; PEL 9780141198910
Romola
PC 9780140434705
Scenes of Clerical Life
PC 9780140436389
Selected Essays, Poems and Other Writings
PC 9780140431483
Silas Marner
PC 9780141439754; PEL 9780141389455

ELLISON, RALPH
The Black Ball
   PM 9780241339220
Flying Home and Other Stories
   PMC 9780241215050
Invisible Man
   PMC 9780141184425
Juneteenth
   PMC 9780241215005

EMECHETA, BUCHI
In the Ditch
   PMC 9780241578124
The Joys of Motherhood
   PMC 9780241578131
Second-Class Citizen
   PMC 9780241532683

EMERSON, RALPH WALDO
Nature
   Great Ideas 9780141036823
Nature and Selected Essays
   PC 9780142437629

EMPSON, WILLIAM
The Complete Poems
   PMC 9780140189629

ENGELS, FRIEDRICH
- *The Communist Manifesto*
  with Karl Marx
  - trans. by Gareth Stedman Jones
  - PC 9780140447576; Pocket HB 9780141395906;
    Great Ideas 9780141018935; LBC 9780141397986
- *The Condition of the Working Class in England*
  - trans. by Florence Kelley-Wischnewetzky
  - PC 9780141191102
- *The Origin of the Family, Private Property and the State*
  - trans. by Alec West
  - PC 9780141191119

English Mystery Plays
- ed. by Peter Happé
- PC 9780140430936

English Romantic Verse
- ed. by David Wright
- PC 9780140421026

The Epic of Gilgamesh
- trans. by Nancy Sandars
- PC 9780140441000
- trans. by Andrew George
- PC 9780140449198

EPICTETUS
- *Discourses and Selected Writings*
    trans. by Robert Dobbin
    PC 9780140449464; Pocket HB 9780241764060
- *Of Human Freedom*
    trans. by Robert Dobbin
    Great Ideas 9780141192352
- *Whatever is Rational is Tolerable*
    trans. by Robert Dobbin
    Archive 9780241752333
- see also *How To Be a Stoic*

EPICURUS
- *The Art of Happiness*
    trans. by George K. Strodach
    PC 9780143107217
- *Being Happy*
    trans. by George K. Strodach
    Great Ideas 9780241473269

EQUIANO, OLAUDAH
- *The Interesting Narrative and Other Writings*
    PC 9780142437162

ERASMUS, DESIDERIUS
- *Praise of Folly*
    trans. by Betty Radice
    PC 9780140446081

ESCHBACH, ANDREAS
The Hair Carpet Weavers
> trans. by Doryl Jensen
> Sci-Fi 9780241454718

ESCHENBACH, WOLFRAM
Parzival
> trans. by A. T. Hatto
> PC 9780140443615

Willehalm
> trans. by Marion E. Gibbs & Sidney M. Johnson
> PC 9780140443998

EURIPIDES
Alcestis and Other Plays
> (*Alcestis, Hippolytus, Iphigenia in Tauris*)
> trans. by Philip Vellacott
> PC 9780140440317

The Bacchae and Other Plays
> (*Ion, The Women of Troy, Helen, The Bacchae*)
> trans. by Philip Vellacott
> PC 9780140440447

The Bacchae and Other Plays
> (*Phoenician Women, Orestes, Bacchae, Iphigenia at Aulis, Rhesus*)
> trans. by John Davie
> PC 9780140447262

Electra and Other Plays
> (*Andromache, Hecabe, Suppliant Women, Electra, Trojan Women*)
> trans. by John Davie
> PC 9780140446685

Heracles and Other Plays
> (*Heracles, Iphigenia Among the Taurians, Ion, Helen, Cyclops*)
> trans. by John Davie
> PC 9780140447255

Medea and Other Plays
> (*Medea, Hecabe, Electra, Heracles*)
> trans. by Philip Vellacott
> PC 9780140441291

Medea and Other Plays
> (*Alcestis, Medea, The Children of Heracles, Hippolytus*)
> trans. by John Davie
> PC 9780140449297

Orestes and Other Plays
> (*The Children of Heracles, Andromache, The Suppliant Women, The Phoenician Women, Orestes, Iphigenia in Aulis*)
> trans. by Philip Vellacott
> PC 9780140442595

see also *Greek Tragedy*

EUSEBIUS
> *The History of the Church from Christ to Constantine*
> trans. by G. A. Williamson, rev. Andrew Louth
> PC 9780140445350

EVANS, WALKER
> with James Agee
> *Let Us Now Praise Famous Men*
> PMC 9780141188492

Eyrbyggja Saga
> trans. by Hermann Pálsson & Paul Edwards
> PC 9780140445305
> see also *Gisli Sursson's Saga* and *The Saga of the People of Eyri*

F

FALLADA, HANS
Alone in Berlin
   trans. by Michael Hofmann
   PMC 9780141189383
Iron Gustav: A Berlin Family Chronicle
   trans. by Philip Owens, rev. Nicholas Jacobs &
   Gardis Cramer von Laue
   PMC 9780141196534
Little Man, What Now?
   trans. by Michael Hofmann
   PMC 9780241300879
Once a Jailbird
   trans. by Eric Sutton, rev. Nicholas Jacobs,
   Gardis Cramer von Laue & Linden Lawson
   PMC 9780141196541
A Small Circus
   trans. by Michael Hofmann
   PMC 9780141196565

Tales from the Underworld
    trans. by Michael Hofmann
    PMC 9780141392851
Why Do You Wear a Cheap Watch?
    trans. by Michael Hofmann
    PM 9780241339244

FALUDY, GYÖRGY
My Happy Days in Hell
    trans. by Kathleen Szasz
    PMC 9780141193205

FANON, FRANTZ
Black Skin, White Masks
    trans. by Richard Philcox
    PMC 9780241396667
The Wretched of the Earth
    trans. by Constance Farrington
    PMC 9780141186542

Fantastic Tales
    ed. by Italo Calvino
    PMC 9780141190129

FEDERICI, SILVIA
Caliban and the Witch: Women, the Body and Primitive Accumulation
    PMC 9780241532539

FERDOWSI, ABOLQASEM
Shahnameh: The Persian Book of Kings
trans. by Dick Davis
PC 9780143108320

FIELDING, HENRY
The History of Tom Jones
PC 9780140436228
Joseph Andrews and *Shamela*
PC 9780140433869

FILIPOWICZ, KORNEL
The Memoir of an Anti-Hero
trans. by Anna Zaranko
PMC 9780241351604

FIORE, QUENTIN
with Marshall McLuhan
The Medium is the Massage
Design 9780141035826

The First Poems in English
trans. by Michael Alexander
PC 9780140433784

FITZGERALD, F. SCOTT
Babylon Revisited
LCC 9780241630839

The Beautiful and Damned
  PMC 9780141187815; HB 9780141194073
The Curious Case of Benjamin Button and Six Other Stories
  PMC 9780141190198
Flappers and Philosophers: The Collected Short Stories
  PMC 9780141192505; HB 9780141194103
The Great Gatsby
  PMC 9780141182636; HB 9780141194059;
  PEL 9780241341469; NS 9780141023434
The Last Tycoon
  PMC 9780141185637; HB 9780141194080
The Rich Boy
  Archive 9780241746271
Tales of the Jazz Age
  HB 9780141197470
Tender is the Night
  PMC 9780141183596; HB 9780141194066;
  PEL 9780241341483
This Side of Paradise
  PMC 9780141185576; HB 9780141194097

Five Revenge Tragedies
  (*The Spanish Tragedy*, *Hamlet*, *Antonio's Revenge*,
  The Tragedy of Hoffman, *The Revenger's Tragedy*)
    ed. by Emma Smith
    PC 9780141192277

FLANNERY, TIM
: *A Warning from the Golden Toad*
: : Green 9780241514436

FLAUBERT, GUSTAVE
: *Flaubert in Egypt*
: : trans. by Francis Steegmuller
: : PC 9780140435825
: *Madame Bovary*
: : trans. by Geoffrey Wall
: : PC 9780140449129; Clothbound 9780141394671
: : trans. by Lydia Davis
: : Deluxe 9780143106494
: *Salammbo*
: : trans. by A. J. Krailsheimer
: : PC 9780140443288
: *Sentimental Education*
: : trans. by Robert Baldick
: : PC 9780140447972
: *A Simple Heart*
: : trans. by Roger Whitehouse
: : LBC 9780141397504
: *Three Tales*
: : trans. by Roger Whitehouse
: : PC 9780140448009

FLEMING, IAN
From Russia with Love
Crime 9780241689363

FORD, FORD MADOX
The Good Soldier
PC 9780141441849
Parade's End
PC 9780241372548

FORD, JOHN
The Broken Heart and *'Tis Pity She's a Whore*
in *The Duchess of Malfi, The White Devil, The Broken Heart and 'Tis Pity She's a Whore*
(see also John Webster)
PC 9780141392233

The Forest of Thieves and the Magic Garden: An Anthology of Medieval Jain Stories
trans. by Phyllis Granoff
PC 9780140455236

FORESTER, C. S.
Payment Deferred
PMC 9780141198101; Crime 9780241654170
Plain Murder
PMC 9780141198132
The Pursued
PMC 9780141198088

FORSTER, E. M.
Aspects of the Novel
  PC 9780141441696
Howards End
  PC 9780141182131; PEL 9780141199405
The Life to Come and Other Stories
  PC 9780241707647
The Longest Journey
  PC 9780141441481
The Machine Stops and Other Stories
  PEL 9780241652572
Maurice
  PC 9780141441139
A Passage to India
  PC 9780241540428
A Room with a View
  PC 9780141183299; PEL 9780141199825
Selected Stories
  PC 9780141186191
Where Angels Fear to Tread
  PC 9780141441450; PEL 9780141199252

FOUCAULT, MICHEL
Aesthetics: Essential Works 1954–1984
  trans. by Robert Hurley et al.
  PMC 9780241435113

Discipline and Punish: The Birth of the Prison
    trans. by Alan Sheridan
    PMC 9780241386019
Ethics: Essential Works 1954–1984
    trans. by Robert Hurley et al.
    PMC 9780241435090
The Foucault Reader
    ed. by Paul Rabinow
    PMC 9780241435144
The History of Sexuality
    trans. by Robert Hurley
    Volume 1: The Will to Knowledge
    PMC 9780241385982
    Volume 2: The Use of Pleasure
    PMC 9780241385999
    Volume 3: The Care of the Self
    PMC 9780241386002
    Volume 4: Confessions of the Flesh
    PMC 9780241389614; HB 9780241389584
Power: Essential Works 1954–1984
    trans. by Robert Hurley et al.
    PMC 9780241435083
Society Must Be Defended
    trans. by David Macey
    PMC 9780241435168

Four French Plays
    (*Cinna, The Misanthrope, Andromache, Phaedra*)
        trans. by John Edmunds
        PC 9780141392080

FRANCE, ANATOLE
The Gods Will Have Blood
    trans. by Frederick Davies
    PC 9780140443523

FRANK, ANNE
The Diary of a Young Girl: The Definitive Edition
    trans. by Susan Massotty
    PC 9780241387481

FRANKLIN, MILES
My Brilliant Career
    Clothbound 9780241699584

FRAZER, JAMES
The Golden Bough
    PMC 9780140189315

FREIRE, PAULO
Pedagogy of the Oppressed
    trans. by Myra Bergman Ramos
    PMC 9780241301111

FREUD, ANNA
Selected Writings
PMC 9780141980911

FREUD, SIGMUND
Beyond the Pleasure Principle
trans. by John Reddick
PMC 9780141184050
Civilization and Its Discontents
trans. by David McLintock
PMC 9780141182360; Pocket HB 9780141395890;
Great Ideas 9780141018997
The Future of an Illusion
trans. by J. A. Underwood & Shaun Whiteside
Great Ideas 9780141036762
Interpreting Dreams
trans. by J. A. Underwood
PMC 9780141187082
The Joke and Its Relation to the Unconscious
trans. by Joyce Crick
PMC 9780141185545
Mass Psychology
trans. by J. A. Underwood
PMC 9780141182414
On Murder, Mourning and Melancholia
trans. by Shaun Whiteside
PMC 9780141183794

An Outline of Psychoanalysis
   trans. by Helena Ragg-Kirkby
   PMC 9780141184043
The Penguin Freud Reader
   ed. by Adam Phillips
   PMC 9780141187433
The Psychology of Love
   trans. by Shaun Whiteside
   PMC 9780141186030
The Psychopathology of Everyday Life
   trans. by Anthea Bell
   PMC 9780141184036
The Schreber Case
   trans. by Andrew Webber
   PMC 9780141183817
Studies in Hysteria
   trans. by Nicola Luckhurst
   PMC 9780141184821
The Uncanny
   trans. by David McLintock
   PMC 9780141182377
The Unconscious
   trans. by Graham Frankland
   PMC 9780141183886
Wild Analysis
   trans. by Alan Bance
   PMC 9780141182421

The 'Wolfman' and Other Cases
    trans. by Louise Adey Huish
    PMC 9780141183800

FRIEDAN, BETTY
The Feminine Mystique
    PMC 9780141192055
The Problem that Has No Name
    PM 9780241339268

FRISCH, MAX
Homo Faber
    trans. by Michael Bullock
    PMC 9780141188669

FROISSART, JEAN
Chronicles
    PC 9780140442007

FUKUOKA, MASANOBU
The Dragonfly Will Be the Messiah
    trans. by Larry Korn
    Green 9780241514443

G

GADDA, CARLO EMILIO
The Experience of Pain
trans. by Richard Dixon
PMC 9780241706992

GAITSKILL, MARY
Bad Behavior
PMC 9780241383100
Because They Wanted To
PMC 9780241464144
Secretary
Archive 9780241752210
Two Girls, Fat and Thin
PMC 9780241464151

GALBRAITH, JOHN KENNETH
The Great Crash 1929
PMC 9780241468081

GALDÓS, BENITO PÉREZ
Fortunata and Jacinta
    trans. by Agnes Gullon
    PC 9780140433050

GALEANO, EDUARDO
Football in Sun and Shadow
    trans. by Mark Fried
    PMC 9780241355350

GALSWORTHY, JOHN
The Forsyte Saga
    Volume 1
    PMC 9780141184180
    Volume 2
    PMC 9780141186832
    Volume 3
    PMC 9780141186849

GANDHI, M. K.
An Autobiography
    PMC 9780141186863

GANJAVI, NEZAMI
Khosrow and Shirin
    trans. by Dick Davis
    PC 9780143138631

Layli and Majnun
    trans. by Dick Davis
    PC 9780143133995

GAO E
The Story of the Stone
    with Cao Xueqin
    trans. by John Minford
    Volume 4: The Debt of Tears
    PC 9780140443714
    Volume 5: The Dreamer Wakes
    PC 9780140443721

GARY, ROMAIN
The Kites
    trans. by Miranda Richmond Mouillot
    PMC 9780241345627
Lady L.
    Archive 9780241752340
Promise at Dawn
    trans. by John Markham Beach
    PMC 9780241347638

GASKELL, ELIZABETH
Cranford
    PC 9780141439884; Clothbound 9780141442549

Cranford / Cousin Phillis
  PC 9780140431049
Gothic Tales
  PC 9780140437416
The Life of Charlotte Brontë
  PC 9780140434934
Lois the Witch
  Archive 9780241746783
Mary Barton
  PC 9780140434644
North and South
  PC 9780140434248; PEL 9780141198927
Ruth
  PC 9780140434309
Sylvia's Lovers
  PC 9780140434224
Wives and Daughters
  PC 9780140434781; PEL 9780141389462

GAUTIER, THEOPHILE
Mademoiselle de Maupin
  trans. by Helen Constantine
  PC 9780140448139

GAWAIN POET, THE
- *Sir Gawain and the Green Knight*
  - ed. by J. A. Burrow
  - PC 9780140422955
  - trans. by Bernard O'Donoghue
  - PC 9780140424539
- *The Works of the Gawain Poet: Sir Gawain and the Green Knight, Pearl, Cleanness, Patience*
  - ed. by Ad Putter & Myra Stokes
  - PC 9780140424140

GAY, JOHN
- *The Beggar's Opera*
  - PC 9780140432206

GEOFFREY OF MONMOUTH
- *The History of the Kings of Britain*
  - trans. by Lewis Thorpe
  - PC 9780140441703

GERALD OF WALES
- *The History and Topography of Ireland*
  - trans. by John O'Meara
  - PC 9780140444230
- *The Journey Through Wales* and *The Description of Wales*
  - trans. by Lewis Thorpe
  - PC 9780140443394

GHOSH, AMITAV
: *Uncanny and Improbable Events*
: : Green 9780141996905

GIBBON, EDWARD
: *The History of the Decline and Fall of the Roman Empire*
: : *Volume I*
: : PC 9780140433937
: : *Volume II*
: : PC 9780140433944
: : *Volume III*
: : PC 9780140433951
: : *Abridged Edition*
: : PC 9780140437645
: *Memoirs of My Life*
: : PC 9780140432176

GIBBON, LEWIS GRASSIC
: *Sunset Song*
: : PC 9780141188409

GIBBONS, STELLA
: *Cold Comfort Farm*
: : PMC 9780241418895

GIBRAN, KAHLIL
: *The Prophet*
: : PMC 9780141187013; HB 9780143133582;
: : LCC 9780241573716

GIDE, ANDRÉ
The Counterfeiters
trans. by Dorothy Bussy
PMC 9780140180930
The Immoralist
trans. by David Watson
PMC 9780141182995
Strait is the Gate
trans. by Dorothy Bussy
PMC 9780141185248

GILBERT, MICHAEL
Game Without Rules
Crime 9780241657744

GILL, ERIC
An Essay on Typography
Design 9780141393568

GILMAN, CHARLOTTE PERKINS
The Yellow Wall-Paper
LBC 9780141397412
The Yellow Wall-Paper, Herland and Selected Writings
PC 9780143105855

GINSBERG, ALLEN
The Best Minds of My Generation: A Literary History of the Beats
PMC 9780141399010

Collected Poems 1947–1997
  PMC 9780141190181
The Essential Ginsberg
  PMC 9780141398990
Howl, Kaddish and Other Poems
  PMC 9780141190167
Selected Poems 1947–1995
  PMC 9780141184760
Sunflower Sutra
  Archive 9780241752180
Television Was a Baby Crawling Toward That Deathchamber
  PM 9780241337622
Wait Till I'm Dead: Poems Uncollected
  PMC 9780141399027
The Yage Letters
with William S. Burroughs
  PMC 9780141189864

GIOVANNI, NIKKI
Poems 1968–2020
  PMC 9780241516447

GIRARD, RENÉ
All Desire is a Desire for Being: Essential Writings
  PC 9780241543238

Gisli Sursson's Saga and *The Saga of the People of Eyri*
    trans. by Judy Quinn & Martin S. Regal
        PC 9780140447729

GISSING, GEORGE
  New Grub Street
    PC 9780140430325
  The Whirlpool
    PC 9780141395647

GLISSANT, ÉDOUARD
  Poetics of Relation
    trans. by Betsy Wing
    PMC 9780241733110

GLÜCK, LOUISE
  Averno
    PMC 9780241526002
  Poems 1962–2020
    PMC 9780241526088

GODWIN, WILLIAM
  Caleb Williams
    PC 9780141441238
  Enquiry Concerning Political Justice and its Influence on Morals and Happiness
    PC 9780141396736

Memoirs of the Author of 'The Rights of Woman'
in *A Short Residence in Sweden* and *Memoirs of the Author of 'The Rights of Woman'*
   (see also Mary Wollstonecraft)
   PC 9780140432695

GOETHE, JOHANN WOLFGANG VON
Elective Affinities
   trans. by R. J. Hollingdale
   PC 9780140442427
Faust
   Part I
   trans. by David Constantine
   PC 9780140449013
   Part II
   trans. by David Constantine
   PC 9780140449020
Italian Journey 1786–1788
   trans. by W. H. Auden & Elizabeth Mayer
   PC 9780140442335
Maxims and Reflections
   trans. by Elisabeth Stopp
   PC 9780140447200
Selected Poetry
   trans. by David Luke
   PC 9780140424560

Sketchy, Doubtful, Incomplete Jottings
   trans. by Elisabeth Stopp
     LBC 9780141397139
The Sorrows of Young Werther
   trans. by Michael Hulse
     PC 9780140445039
see also *Romantic Fairy Tales*

GOFFMAN, ERVING
   Asylums: Essays on the Social Situation of Mental Patients and Other Inmates
     PMC 9780241548004
   The Presentation of Self in Everyday Life
     PMC 9780241547991
   Stigma: Notes on the Management of Spoiled Identity
     PMC 9780241548011

GOGOL, NIKOLAI
   Dead Souls
     trans. by Robert Maguire
     PC 9780140448078
   The Diary of a Madman, The Government Inspector and Selected Stories
     trans. by Ronald Wilks
     PC 9780140449075

The Night Before Christmas
>trans. by Anna Summers
>HB 9780143122487

The Nose
>trans. by Ronald Wilks
>LBC 9780141397528

The Golden Age of British Short Stories 1890–1914
>ed. by Philip Hensher
>PC 9780241434314

GOLDSMITH, OLIVER
The Vicar of Wakefield
>PC 9780140431599

GONCHAROV, IVAN
Oblomov
>trans. by David Magarshack
>PC 9780140449877

GORKY, MAXIM
My Childhood
>trans. by Ronald Wilks
>PMC 9780140182859

GORODISCHER, ANGÉLICA
Trafalgar
>trans. by Amalia Gladhart
>Sci-Fi 9780241467961

GOSSE, EDMUND
Father and Son
PMC 9780140182767

GOTTFRIED VON STRASSBURG
Tristan
in *Tristan with the 'Tristran' of Thomas*
trans. by A. T. Hatto
(see also Thomas of Britain)
PC 9780140440980

GRACE, PATRICIA
Potiki
PMC 9780241413555

GRACIÁN, BALTASAR
How to Use Your Enemies
trans. by Jeremy Robbins
LBC 9780141398273
The Pocket Oracle and Art of Prudence
trans. by Jeremy Robbins
PC 9780141442457

GRAHAM, BILLY
with Don McGregor, Rich Buckler, Stan Lee & Jack Kirby
Black Panther
Marvel 9780143135814; Marvel HB 9780143135807

GRAHAME, KENNETH
: *The Wind in the Willows*
: PC 9780143039099; Deluxe 9780143106647

GRANT, ULYSSES S.
: *Personal Memoirs of Ulysses S. Grant*
: PC 9780140437010

GRAVES, ROBERT
: *The Anger of Achilles: The Iliad*
: PC 9780140455601
: *Claudius the God*
: PMC 9780141188607
: *The Complete Poems*
: PMC 9780141182063
: *Complete Short Stories*
: PMC 9780141189451
: *Count Belisarius*
: PMC 9780141188133
: *The Golden Fleece*
: PMC 9780141197647
: *Goodbye to All That*
: PMC 9780141184593
: *Homer's Daughter*
: PMC 9780141197661
: *I, Claudius*
: PMC 9780141188591

King Jesus
  PMC 9780141197654
Sergeant Lamb of the Ninth
  PMC 9780141197685
Seven Days in New Crete
  PMC 9780141197678
Wife to Mr Milton
  PMC 9780141197500

Great Italian Stories: 10 Parallel Texts
  ed. by Jhumpa Lahiri
  Parallel 9780241634455

Great Japanese Stories: 10 Parallel Texts
  ed. by Jay Rubin
  Parallel 9780241634479

Great Spanish Stories: 10 Parallel Texts
  ed. by Margaret Jull Costa
  Parallel 9780241662199

The Greek Alexander Romance
  trans. by Richard Stoneman
  PC 9780140445602

Greek Fiction: Callirhoe, Daphnis and Chloe, Letters of Chion
  trans. by Rosanna Omitowoju, Phiroze Vasunia & John Penwill
  PC 9780140449259

The Greek Sophists
    trans. by John Dillon & Tania Gergel
    PC 9780140436891

Greek Tragedy
    ed. by Shomit Dutta
    PC 9780141439365

GREEN, G. F.
In the Making
    PMC 9780141197579

GREEN, JULIAN
Paris
    PMC 9780141194653

GREENBERG, JOANNE
I Never Promised You a Rose Garden
    PMC 9780241563427
In This Sign
    PMC 9780241679098

GREGORY OF TOURS
The History of the Franks
    trans. by Lewis Thorpe
    PC 9780140442953

GRIMM, THE BROTHERS
Selected Tales
   trans. by David Luke
   PC 9780140444018
Grimm Tales for Young and Old
   retold by Philip Pullman
   PC 9780141442228; Clothbound 9780241472729

GRIMMELSHAUSEN, HANS JAKOB CHRISTOFFEL VON
The Adventures of Simplicius Simplicissimus
   trans. by J. A. Underwood
   PC 9780241309865

GROSSMITH, GEORGE & WEEDON
The Diary of a Nobody
   PC 9780140437324

GRUBB, DAVIS
The Night of the Hunter
   Crime 9780241640425

GUEVARA, ERNESTO CHE
The Bolivian Diary
   trans. by the Che Guevara Studies Center
   PMC 9780241465073

Guerrilla Warfare
   trans. by the Che Guevara Studies Center
   PMC 9780241465080
I Embrace You With All My Revolutionary Fervor: Letters 1947–1967
   trans. by Ocean Press
   PMC 9780241465127
The Motorcycle Diaries
   trans. by the Che Guevara Studies Center
   PMC 9780241465103
Reminiscences of the Cuban Revolutionary War
   trans. by the Che Guevara Studies Center
   PMC 9780241465097

GURDJIEFF, G. I.
Meetings with Remarkable Men
   trans. by A. R. Orage
   PMC 9780141394497

GURNEY, IVOR
with Wilfred Owen & Isaac Rosenberg
Three Poets of the First World War
   PC 9780141182070

GUSTON, PHILIP
I Paint What I Want to See
   Design 9780241525715

GUTHRIE, WOODY
  Bound for Glory
    PMC 9780141187228

H

HACKETT, PAT
  with Andy Warhol
  POPism
    PMC 9780141189420

HAFEZ
  Faces of Love
  with Jahan Malek Khatun & Obayd-e Zakani
    trans. by Dick Davis
    Deluxe 9780143107286
  I am a Bird from Paradise
    trans. by Dick Davis
    Archive 9780241747254
  The Nightingales are Drunk
    trans. by Dick Davis
    LBC 9780141980263

HAGGARD, H. RIDER
  King Solomon's Mines
    PC 9780141439525

She
　PC 9780140437638

HAKLUYT, RICHARD
Voyages and Discoveries
　PC 9780140430738

HALL, RADCLYFFE
The Well of Loneliness
　PMC 9780141191836

HAMILTON, ALEXANDER
with John Jay & James Madison
The Federalist Papers
　PC 9780140444957

HAMMETT, DASHIELL
The Thin Man
　PMC 9780141194608

HANDKE, PETER
The Goalkeeper's Anxiety at the Penalty Kick
　trans. by Michael Roloff
　PMC 9780241457696
The Left-Handed Woman
　trans. by Ralph Manheim
　PMC 9780241457672

Repetition
   trans. by Ralph Manheim
   PMC 9780241457689

HARDY, THOMAS
Desperate Remedies
   PC 9780140435238
The Distracted Preacher and Other Tales
   PC 9780140431247
Far From the Madding Crowd
   PC 9780141439655; Clothbound 9780141393384;
   PEL 9780141198934
The Fiddler of the Reels and Other Stories 1888–1900
   PC 9780140439007
The Hand of Ethelberta
   PC 9780140435023
Jude the Obscure
   PC 9780140435382; Clothbound 9780241382691
A Laodicean
   PC 9780140435061
The Mayor of Casterbridge
   PC 9780141439785; Clothbound 9780241347775
A Pair of Blue Eyes
   PC 9780140435290
The Pursuit of the Well-Beloved and *The Well-Beloved*
   PC 9780140435191

The Return of the Native
    PC 9780140435184
Selected Poems
    PC 9780140433418
Tess of the D'Urbervilles
    PC 9780141439594; Clothbound 9780141040332;
    PEL 9780141199948
The Trumpet-Major
    PC 9780140435405
Two on a Tower
    PC 9780140435368; PEL 9780141199436
Under the Greenwood Tree
    PC 9780140435535
Wessex Poems and Other Verses
    Clothbound Poetry 9780241303139
The Withered Arm and Other Stories 1874–1888
    PC 9780140435320
The Woodlanders
    PC 9780140435474

HARRISON, HARRY
Make Room! Make Room!
    PMC 9780141190235; Sci-Fi 9780241507704

HARTLEY, L. P.
Facial Justice
    PMC 9780141395067

The Go-Between
　PMC 9780141187785

HAŠEK, JAROSLAV
The Good Soldier Švejk
　trans. by Cecil Parrott
　PC 9780140449914

HAWTHORNE, NATHANIEL
The House of the Seven Gables
　PC 9780140390056
The Scarlet Letter
　PC 9780143107668; PEL 9780141199450

HAYES, ALFRED
The Girl on the Via Flaminia
　PMC 9780241342329
My Face for the World to See
　PMC 9780241342305

HAZLITT, WILLIAM
The Fight and Other Writings
　PC 9780140436136
On the Pleasure of Hating
　Great Ideas 9780141018928

HEALY, JOHN
The Grass Arena
　PMC 9780141189598

HEARN, LAFCADIO
Japanese Ghost Stories
PC 9780241381274; NS 9780241675298
Of Ghosts and Goblins
LCC 9780241573723
Some Japanese Ghosts
Archive 9780241746875

HEATH, ROY
The Murderer
PMC 9780241552728

HEBEL, JOHANN PETER
The Treasure Chest
trans. by John Hibberd
PC 9780140446395

HECK, DON
The Avengers
with Stan Lee, Jack Kirby, Roy Thomas,
John Buscema & Sal Buscema
Marvel 9780143135791; Marvel HB 9780143135784
X-Men
with Stan Lee, Jack Kirby, Roy Thomas, Werner
Roth & Neal Adams
Marvel 9780143135777; Marvel HB 9780143135760

HEDAYAT, SADEQ
Blind Owl
trans. by Sassan Tabatabai
PC 9780143136583

HEGEL, GEORG
Introductory Lectures on Aesthetics
trans. by Bernard Bosanquet
PC 9780140433357

HEINE, HEINRICH
The Harz Journey and Selected Prose
trans. by Ritchie Robertson
PC 9780140448504
Selected Verse
trans. by Peter Branscombe
PC 9780140420982

HEISENBERG, WERNER
Physics and Philosophy
PMC 9780141182155

HÉLOÏSE D'ARGENTEUIL
with Abelard, Peter
The Letters of Abelard and Heloise
trans. by Betty Radice
PC 9780140448993

HENRI, ADRIAN
  with Roger McGough & Brian Patten
  The Mersey Sound
    PMC 9780141189260

HENRY, O.
  The Cop and the Anthem and Other Stories
    PEL 9780241447468
  The Gift of the Magi
    LCC 9780241597019
  Selected Stories
    PC 9780140186888

HERBERT, GEORGE
  The Complete Poetry
    PC 9780141392042
  The Temple
    Clothbound Poetry 9780241303078

HERBERT, ZBIGNIEW
  Selected Poems
    PMC 9780241654613

HERODOTUS
  The Histories
    trans. by Aubrey de Sélincourt
    PC 9780140449082
    trans. by Tom Holland
    PC 9780140455397
  see also *On Writing History*

HERSEY, JOHN
Hiroshima
   PMC 9780141184371

HERUKA, TSANGNYÖN
The Life of Milarepa
   trans. by Andrew Quintman
   PC 9780143106227

HESIOD
Theogony and *Works and Days*
in *Hesiod and Theognis*
   trans. by Dorothea Wender
   (see also Theognis)
   PC 9780140442830
Works and Days
   trans. by A. E. Stallings
   PC 9780141197524

HESSE, HERMANN
Narcissus and Goldmund
   trans. by Leila Vennewitz
   PMC 9780141984612
Steppenwolf
   trans. by David Horrocks
   PMC 9780141192093

Strange News from Another Planet
   trans. by Jack Zipes
   Archive 9780241752074

HIJUELOS, OSCAR
The Mambo Kings Play Songs of Love
   PMC 9780141189666

HILDEGARD OF BINGEN
Selected Writings
   trans. by Mark Atherton
   PC 9780140436044

HIMES, CHESTER
All God's Chillun Got Pride
   Archive 9780241752104
All Shot Up
   PMC 9780241521120
The Big Gold Dream
   PMC 9780241692622
Blind Man with a Pistol
   PMC 9780241692615
Cotton Comes to Harlem
   PMC 9780241521090; Crime 9780241639221
The Crazy Kill
   PMC 9780241692639
The Heat's On
   PMC 9780241521106

If He Hollers, Let Him Go
    PMC 9780241692424
A Rage in Harlem
    PMC 9780241521083
The Real Cool Killers
    PMC 9780241521113
Yesterday Will Make You Cry
    PMC 9780241692646

Hindu Myths
    trans. by Wendy Doniger
    PC 9780140449907

HINES, BARRY
A Kestrel for a Knave
    PMC 9780141184982

HINTON, S. E.
The Outsiders
    PMC 9780141189116

Hippocratic Writings
    trans. by J. Chadwick, W. N. Mann, I. M. Lonie & E. T. Withington
    PC 9780140444513

HOBAN, RUSSELL
Fremder
    PMC 9780241485699

Kleinzeit
   PMC 9780241485705
The Lion of Boaz-Jachin and Jachin-Boaz
   PMC 9780241485712
The Medusa Frequency
   PMC 9780241485729
Mr Rinyo-Clacton's Offer
   PMC 9780241485736
Pilgermann
   PMC 9780241485743
Riddley Walker
   PMC 9780241485750
Turtle Diary
   PMC 9780241485767

HOBBES, THOMAS
Leviathan
   PC 9780141395098

HOFFMANN, E. T. A.
The Life and Opinions of the Tomcat Murr
   trans. by Anthea Bell
   PC 9780140446319
The Nutcracker
   trans. by Joachim Neugroschel, R. J. Hollingdale & Sally Hayward
   HB 9780143122500; LCC 9780241597064

Tales of Hoffmann
>trans. by R. J. Hollingdale, Stella Humphries,
>Vernon Humphries & Sally Hayward
>PC 9780140443929

HOGG, JAMES
The Private Memoirs and Confessions of a Justified Sinner
>PC 9780141441535

HOGGART, RICHARD
The Uses of Literacy: Aspects of Working-Class Life
>PMC 9780141191584

HOLBEIN, HANS
The Dance of Death
>ed. by Ulinka Rublack
>PC 9780141396828

HÖLDERLIN, FRIEDRICH
Essays and Letters
>trans. by Jeremy Adler & Charlie Louth
>PC 9780140447088
Selected Poems and Fragments
>trans. by Michael Hamburger
>PC 9780140424164

HOLIDAY, BILLIE
Lady Sings the Blues
>PMC 9780241351291

HOLMES, JOHN CLELLON
Go
PMC 9780141188393

HOMER
Circe and the Cyclops
trans. by Robert Fagles
LBC 9780141398617
The Homeric Hymns
trans. by Nicholas Richardson
PC 9780140437829
The Iliad
trans. by E. V. Rieu, rev. Peter Jones &
D. C. H. Rieu
PC 9780140447941; Clothbound 9780141394657
trans. by Robert Graves (as *The Anger of Achilles*)
PC 9780140455601
trans. by Martin Hammond
PC 9780140444445
trans. by Robert Fagles
PC 9780140445923; Deluxe 9780140275360

The Odyssey
    trans. by E. V. Rieu, rev. D. C. H. Rieu
    PC 9780140449112; Clothbound 9780141192444
    trans. by Robert Fagles
    PC 9780143039952; Deluxe 9780140268867
    trans. by Daniel Mendelsohn
    HB 9780241733585
The Wrath of Achilles
    trans. by E. V. Rieu, rev. Peter Jones &
    D. C. H. Rieu
    Archive 9780241746943

HOOKS, BELL
Art on My Mind: Visual Politics
    PMC 9780241711491

HOPKINS, GERARD MANLEY
Poems and Prose
    PC 9780140420159

HORACE
The Complete Odes and Epodes
    trans. by W. G. Shepherd
    PC 9780140444223

Satires and *Epistles*
in *The Satires of Horace and Persius*
   trans. by Niall Rudd
   (see also Persius)
   PC 9780140455083
   see also *Classical Literary Criticism*

HORNBY, NICK
Fever Pitch
   PMC 9780141391816

HORNUNG, E. W.
Raffles, Gentleman Thief
   PC 9780241790229

HOUSMAN, A. E.
A Shropshire Lad
   Clothbound Poetry 9780241303153
A Shropshire Lad and Other Poems
   PC 9780140424744

How To Be a Stoic
   trans. by C. D. N. Costa, Robert Dobbin &
   Martin Hammond
   Great Ideas 9780241475263

HOYLE, FRED
The Black Cloud
   PMC 9780141196404

HRABAL, BOHUMIL
All My Cats
trans. by Paul Wilson
PMC 9780241422199
Closely Watched Trains
trans. by Edith Pargeter
PMC 9780241290224; Archive 9780241752142
Cutting It Short
trans. by James Naughton
PMC 9780241290262
The Little Town Where Time Stood Still
trans. by James Naughton
PMC 9780241290248

Hrafnkel's Saga and Other Icelandic Stories
trans. by Hermann Pálsson
PC 9780140442380

HUDSON, W. H.
A Shepherd's Life
PC 9780241273357

HUGHES, DOROTHY B.
In a Lonely Place
PMC 9780141192314; Crime 9780241639184

HUGO, VICTOR
- *Les Misérables*
    - trans. by Norman Denny
    - Clothbound 9781846140495
    - trans. by Christine Donougher
    - PC 9780241248744
- *Notre-Dame de Paris*
    - trans. by John Sturrock
    - PC 9780140443530

HUMBOLDT, ALEXANDER VON
- *Personal Narrative of a Journey to the Equinoctial Regions of the New Continent*
    - trans. by Jason Wilson
    - PC 9780140445534

HUME, DAVID
- *Complete Essays*
    - *Volume 1*
    - HB 9780241730874
    - *Volume 2*
    - HB 9780241730867
- *Dialogues Concerning Natural Religion*
    - PC 9780140445367
- *On Suicide*
    - Great Ideas 9780141023953
- *A Treatise of Human Nature*
    - PC 9780140432442

HUXLEY, ELSPETH
Red Strangers
PMC 9780141188508

HUYSMANS, JORIS-KARL
Against Nature (À Rebours)
trans. by Robert Baldick
PC 9780140447637
The Damned (Là-Bas)
trans. by Terry Hale
PC 9780140447675

I

I Ching
    trans. by John Minford
    Deluxe 9780143106920

IBN FADLĀN
Ibn Fadlān and the Land of Darkness: Arab Travellers in the Far North
    trans. by Paul Lunde & Caroline E. M. Stone
    PC 9780140455076

IBN HAJAR AL-'ASQALANI
Merits of the Plague
    trans. by Joel Blecher & Mairaj Syed
    PC 9780143136613

IBN MUHAMMAD AL-WAZZAN, AL-HASAN
see Leo Africanus

IBN MUNQIDH, USAMA
The Book of Contemplation: Islam and the Crusades
    trans. by Paul M. Cobb
    PC 9780140455137

IBSEN, HENRIK
A Doll's House and Other Plays
(A Doll's House, Ghosts, Pillars of the Community, An Enemy of the People)
trans. by Deborah Dawkin & Erik Skuggevik
PC 9780141194561

An Enemy of the People
adapted by Arthur Miller
PMC 9780241198865

Ghosts and Other Plays
(Ghosts, A Public Enemy, When We Dead Wake)
trans. by Peter Watts
PC 9780140441352

Hedda Gabler and Other Plays
(The Wild Duck, Rosmersholm, The Lady from the Sea, Hedda Gabbler)
trans. by Deborah Dawkin & Erik Skuggevik
PC 9780141194578

The Master Builder and Other Plays
(The Master Builder, Little Eyolf, John Gabriel Borkman, When We Dead Awaken)
trans. by Barbara Haveland & Anne-Marie Stanton-Ife
PC 9780141194592

Peer Gynt and *Brand*
trans. by Geoffrey Hill
PC 9780141197586

IGNATIUS OF LOYOLA
Personal Writings
trans. by Joseph Munitiz & Philip Endean
PC 9780140433852

Imagist Poetry
ed. by Peter Jones
PMC 9780141185705

INCHBALD, ELIZABETH
A Simple Story
PC 9780140434736

Inspirations: Selections from Classic Literature
ed. by Paulo Coelho
PC 9780141442495

IONESCO, EUGENE
Rhinoceros, The Chairs, The Lesson
trans. by Derek Prouse & Donald Watson
PMC 9780141184296

IRVING, WASHINGTON
The Legend of Sleepy Hollow and Other Stories
PC 9780143107538

Islamic Mystical Poetry: Sufi Verse from the early Mystics to Rumi
trans. by Mahmood Jamal
PC 9780140424737

J

JACKSON, SHIRLEY
The Bird's Nest
PMC 9780141391946
The Daemon Lover
Archive 9780241752135
Dark Tales
PMC 9780241308493
Hangsaman
PMC 9780141391984
The Haunting of Hill House
PMC 9780141191447; Clothbound 9780241689646;
HB 9780143122357
Just an Ordinary Day
PMC 9780141983202
Let Me Tell You
PMC 9780241198209
Life Among the Savages
PMC 9780241387801
The Lottery
LCC 9780241590539

The Lottery and Other Stories
  PMC 9780141191430
The Missing Girl
  PM 9780241339282
Raising Demons
  PMC 9780241473009
The Road Through the Wall
  PMC 9780141392004
The Sundial
  PMC 9780141391960
We Have Always Lived in the Castle
  PMC 9780141191454; Crime 9780241685044

JACOBO DI VORAGINE
The Golden Legend
  trans. by Christopher Stace
  PC 9780140446487

JACOBS, HARRIET
Incidents in the Life of a Slave Girl, Written by Herself
  PC 9780140437959

JAFFE, RONA
The Best of Everything
  PMC 9780141196312

JAMES, C. L. R.
> *The Black Jacobins: Toussaint L'Ouverture and the San Domingo Revolution*
> > PMC 9780241562079

JAMES, HENRY
> *The Ambassadors*
> > PC 9780141441320
> *The American*
> > PC 9780140390827
> *The Aspern Papers and Other Tales*
> > PC 9780141389790
> *The Awkward Age*
> > PC 9780140432978
> *The Bostonians*
> > PC 9780140437669
> *Daisy Miller*
> > PC 9780141441344
> *Daisy Miller and Other Tales*
> > PC 9780141389776
> *Daisy Miller* and *The Turn of the Screw*
> > PEL 9780141199757
> *The Europeans*
> > PC 9780141441405
> *The Figure in the Carpet*
> > LBC 9780141397580

The Golden Bowl
 PC 9780141441276
A Life in Letters
 PC 9780140435160
The Portrait of a Lady
 PC 9780141441269; Clothbound 9780141394664;
 PEL 9780141199122
The Princess Casamassima
 PC 9780140432541
Roderick Hudson
 PC 9780140432640
The Spoils of Poynton
 PC 9780140432886
The Tragic Muse
 PC 9780140433890
The Turn of the Screw
 PC 9780141441351
The Turn of the Screw and Other Ghost Stories
 PC 9780141389752; Clothbound 9780241552650
Washington Square
 PC 9780141441368
What Maisie Knew
 PC 9780141441375
The Wings of the Dove
 PC 9780141441283

JAMES, M. R.

Count Magnus and Other Ghost Stories
PC 9780143039396

Ghost Stories
PEL 9780241341629

The Haunted Dolls' House and Other Ghost Stories
PC 9780143039921

The Stalls of Barchester Cathedral
Archive 9780241746745

JAMES, WILLIAM

Pragmatism and Other Writings
PC 9780140437355

The Varieties of Religious Experience
PC 9780140390346

Japanese Nō Dramas
trans. by Royall Tyler
PC 9780140445398

JAY, JOHN
with Alexander Hamilton & James Madison

The Federalist Papers
PC 9780140444957

JEROME, JEROME K.

Three Men in a Boat
PC 9780141441214

Three Men in a Boat and *Three Men on the Bummel*
    PC 9780140437508

JEWETT, SARAH ORNE
The Country of the Pointed Firs
    Archive 9780241752203
The Country of the Pointed Firs and Other Stories
    PC 9780140434767

JOAQUIN, NICK
The Woman Who Had Two Navels and Tales of the Tropical Gothic
    PC 9780143130710

JOHNSON, SAMUEL
A Dictionary of the English Language: An Anthology
    PC 9780141441573
The History of Rasselas, Prince of Abissinia
    PC 9780141439709
A Journey to the Western Islands
in *A Journey to the Western Islands of Scotland* and *The Journal of a Tour to the Hebrides*
    (see also James Boswell)
    PC 9780140432213
Selected Essays
    PC 9780140436273

JOINVILLE, JOHN OF
   with Geoffrey of Villehardouin
   Chronicles of the Crusades
      trans. by Caroline Smith
      PC 9780140449983

JONES, JAMES
   From Here to Eternity
      PMC 9780141393223
   The Thin Red Line
      PMC 9780141393247

JONSON, BEN
   The Complete Poems
      PC 9780140422771
   Volpone and Other Plays
      PC 9780141441184

JORDAN, ELIZABETH GARVER
   The Case of Lizzie Borden and Other Writings
      PC 9780143137603

JORDAN, JUNE
   The Essential June Jordan
      PMC 9780241508718
   Passion
      Archive 9780241752425

JOSEPHUS
- *The Jewish War*
    - trans. by G. A. Williamson, rev. E. Mary Smallwood
    - PC 9780140444209

JOYCE, JAMES
- *Dubliners*
    - PMC 9780141182452; Clothbound 9780241720202; PEL 9780141199627; Deluxe 9780143107453
- *Finnegans Wake*
    - PMC 9780141183114
- *A Portrait of the Artist as a Young Man*
    - PMC 9780141182667; Deluxe 9780143108245
- *Ulysses*
    - PMC 9780141182803; Clothbound 9780241552636
- *Ulysses: Annotated Students' Edition*
    - PMC 9780141197418

JULIAN OF NORWICH
- *Revelations of Divine Love*
    - trans. by Elizabeth Spearing
    - PC 9780140446739

JÜNGER, ERNST
- *Storm of Steel*
    - trans. by Michael Hofmann
    - PMC 9780141186917

JUSTINIAN
The Digest of Roman Law: Theft, Rapine, Damage and Insult
trans. by C. F. Kolbert
PC 9780140443431

JUVENAL
The Sixteen Satires
trans. by Peter Green
PC 9780140447040

The Kabbalistic Tradition: An Anthology of Jewish Mysticism
    trans. by Alan Unterman
    PC 9780140437997

KAFKA, FRANZ
  Amerika
    trans. by Michael Hofmann
    PC 9780241372586
  The Burrow and Other Stories
    trans. by Michael Hofmann
    PC 9780241372593
  The Castle
    trans. by J. A. Underwood
    PC 9780241678916; PMC 9780241197806
  The Diaries of Franz Kafka
    trans. by Ross Benjamin
    PC 9780241695753

A Hunger-Artist
    trans. by Michael Hofmann
    Archive 9780241746929

Investigations of a Dog
    trans. by Michael Hofmann
    PM 9780241339305

Metamorphosis
    trans. by Michael Hofmann
    LCC 9780241573730

Metamorphosis and Other Stories
    trans. by Michael Hofmann
    PC 9780241372555; PMC 9780241436240;
    Deluxe 9780143105244

The Trial
    trans. by Idris Parry
    PC 9780241678893; PMC 9780241197790

Kalevala: The Epic of the Finnish People
    trans. by Eino Friberg
    PC 9780241403068

Kama Sutra: A Guide to the Art of Pleasure
    trans. by A. N. D. Haksar
    PC 9780140455588

KANDINSKY, WASSILY
    Concerning the Spiritual in Art
        trans. by Ruth Ahmedzai Kemp
        PC 9780241384800

KANG, YOUNGHILL
East Goes West
PC 9780143134305

KANT, IMMANUEL
An Answer to the Question: 'What Is Enlightenment?'
trans. by H. B. Nisbet
Great Ideas 9780141043883
Critique of Pure Reason
trans. by Max Müller, rev. Marcus Weigelt
PC 9780140447477

KANUTE, BANNA
with Bamba Suso
Sunjata: Gambian Versions of the Mande Epic
trans. by Gordon Innes & Bakari Sidibe
PC 9780140447361

KAPUŚCIŃSKI, RYSZARD
Another Day of Life
trans. by William R. Brand & Katarzyna Mroczkowska-Brand
PMC 9780141186788
The Emperor
trans. by William R. Brand & Katarzyna Mroczkowska-Brand
PMC 9780141188034

Nobody Leaves: Impressions of Poland
    trans. by William R. Brand
    PMC 9780718192006
Shah of Shahs
    trans. by William R. Brand & Katarzyna Mroczkowska-Brand
    PMC 9780141188041

KARKAVITSAS, ANDREAS
The Archeologist and Selected Sea Stories
    trans. by Johanna Hanink
    PC 9780143136248

KARSKI, JAN
Story of a Secret State: My Report to the World
    PMC 9780241407387

KAVANAGH, PATRICK
Collected Poems
    PMC 9780141186931
The Great Hunger
    PM 9780241339343
The Green Fool
    PMC 9780141184203
Selected Poems
    PMC 9780141183480
Tarry Flynn
    PMC 9780141183619

KAWABATA, YASUNARI
  Beauty and Sadness
    trans. by Howard Hibbett
    PMC 9780141192611
  Dandelions
    trans. by Michael Emmerich
    PMC 9780241367186
  The Rainbow
    trans. by Haydn Trowell
    PMC 9780241542293
  Snow Country
    trans. by Edward G. Seidensticker
    PMC 9780141192598; LCC 9780241597361
  The Sound of the Mountain
    trans. by Edward G. Seidensticker
    PMC 9780141192628
  Thousand Cranes
    trans. by Edward G. Seidensticker
    PMC 9780141192604; Archive 9780241752098

KEATING, H. R. F.
  The Perfect Murder: The First Inspector Ghote Mystery
    PMC 9780141194479

KEATS, JOHN
  The Complete Poems
    PC 9780140422108

Lamia, Isabella, The Eve of St Agnes and Other Poems
  Clothbound Poetry 9780241303146
Selected Letters
  PC 9780141192796
Selected Poems
  PC 9780140424478
So Bright and Delicate: Love Letters and Poems of John Keats to Fanny Brawne
  PC 9780141442471

KEMPE, MARGERY
The Book of Margery Kempe
  trans. by Barry Windeatt
  PC 9780140432510

KENKŌ, YOSHIDA
A Cup of Sake Beneath the Cherry Trees
  trans. by Meredith McKinney
  LBC 9780141398259
Essays in Idleness
in *Essays in Idleness* and *Hōjōki*
  trans. by Meredith McKinney
  (see also Kamo no Chōmei)
  PC 9780141192109

KEROUAC, JACK
And the Hippos Were Boiled in Their Tanks
with William S. Burroughs
PMC 9780141189673
Big Sur
PMC 9780141198255; NS 9780241348086
Desolation Angels
PMC 9780141198262
The Dharma Bums
PMC 9780141184883; Deluxe 9780143039600;
NS 9780241348062
Doctor Sax
PMC 9780141198248
The Haunted Life
PMC 9780141394091
Lonesome Traveler
PMC 9780141184906; NS 9780241348079
Maggie Cassidy
PMC 9780141190037
Mexico City Blues
PMC 9780241388945
On the Road
PMC 9780141182674; Clothbound 9780241552643;
NS 9780241347959
On the Road: The Original Scroll
PMC 9780141189215

Pic
   PMC 9780241388969
Piers of the Homeless Night
   PM 9780241339183
Satori in Paris
   PMC 9780141198231
The Sea is My Brother: The Lost Novel
   PMC 9780141193342
The Subterraneans
   PMC 9780141184890
The Town and the City
   PMC 9780141182230
Tristessa
   PMC 9780241388990; Archive 9780241752067
Vanity of Duluoz
   PMC 9780141198217
Visions of Cody
   PMC 9780141198224
Visions of Gerard
   PMC 9780241389010
Wake Up
   PMC 9780141189468

KESEY, KEN
One Flew Over the Cuckoo's Nest
   PMC 9780141187884; Deluxe 9780143105022

KEUN, IRMGARD
After Midnight
trans. by Anthea Bell
PMC 9780241391822; Archive 9780241747285
The Artificial Silk Girl
trans. by Kathie von Ankum
PMC 9780241382967
Child of All Nations
trans. by Michael Hofmann
PMC 9780141188454
Ferdinand, the Man with the Kind Heart
trans. by Michael Hofmann
PMC 9780241441336
Gilgi, One of Us
trans. by Geoff Wilkes
PMC 9780241391808

KEYNES, JOHN MAYNARD
The Essential Keynes
PC 9781846148132

KHATUN, JAHAN MALEK
with Hafez & Obayd-e Zakani
Faces of Love
trans. by Dick Davis
Deluxe 9780143107286

KHAYYAM, OMAR
The Ruba'iyat of Omar Khayyam
trans. by Peter Avery & John Heath-Stubbs
PC 9780140443844

KHUSRAU, AMIR
A Tale of Four Dervishes
trans. by Mir Amman
PC 9780140455182

KIERKEGAARD, SØREN
Either/Or: A Fragment of Life
trans. by Alastair Hannay
PC 9780140445770
Fear and Trembling
trans. by Alastair Hannay
PC 9780140444490; Pocket HB 9780141395883;
Great Ideas 9780141023939
A Literary Review
trans. by Alastair Hannay
PC 9780140448016
Papers and Journals
trans. by Alastair Hannay
PC 9780140445893
The Sickness Unto Death
trans. by Alastair Hannay
PC 9780140445336; Great Ideas 9780141036656

The Seducer's Diary
    trans. by Alastair Hannay
    Archive 9780241752173

KIM MAN-JUNG
The Nine Cloud Dream
    trans. by Heinz Insu Fenkl
    PC 9780143131274

KIM RONYOUNG
Clay Walls
    PC 9780143138242

KIMMERER, ROBIN WALL
The Democracy of Species
    Green 9780141997049

KING, JR., MARTIN LUTHER
A Gift of Love
    PMC 9780141985183
Letter from Birmingham Jail
    PM 9780241339466
A Tough Mind and a Tender Heart
    Great Ideas 9780241473252
Why We Can't Wait
    PMC 9780241345443

KING, SHERWOOD
If I Die Before I Wake
PMC 9780141192192

KINGSLEY, CHARLES
The Water Babies: A Fairy Tale for a Land-Baby
PC 9780143105091

KINGSLEY, MARY
Travels in West Africa
PC 9780141439426

KIPLING, RUDYARD
The Jungle Books
PC 9780141196657; Clothbound 9780141394626
Just So Stories
PC 9780141442402
Kim
PC 9780141442372; PEL 9780141199979
The Man Who Would Be King: Selected Stories
PC 9780141442358
Plain Tales from the Hills
PC 9780141442396
Selected Poems
PC 9780140424317

KIRBY, JACK
- *The Avengers*
  with Stan Lee, Roy Thomas, Don Heck, John Buscema & Sal Buscema
  Marvel 9780143135791; Marvel HB 9780143135784
- *Black Panther*
  with Don McGregor, Rich Buckler, Billy Graham & Stan Lee
  Marvel 9780143135814; Marvel HB 9780143135807
- *Captain America*
  with Joe Simon, Stan Lee, Jim Steranko & John Romita Sr.
  Marvel 9780143135753; Marvel HB 9780143135746
- *Fantastic Four*
  with Stan Lee
  Marvel 9780143135838; Marvel HB 9780143135821
- *X-Men*
  with Stan Lee, Roy Thomas, Werner Roth, Don Heck & Neal Adams
  Marvel 9780143135777; Marvel HB 9780143135760

KIŠ, DANILO
- *The Encyclopedia of the Dead*
  trans. by Michael Henry Heim, rev. Mark Thompson
  PMC 9780141396989

The Legend of the Sleepers
    trans. by Michael Henry Heim, rev. Mark Thompson
    PM 9780241339374

KLEIN, NAOMI
Hot Money
    Green 9780141996882

KLEIST, HEINRICH
The Marquise of O— and Other Stories
    trans. by David Luke & Nigel Reeves
    PC 9780140443592

KOESTLER, ARTHUR
The Sleepwalkers: A History of Man's Changing Vision of the Universe
    PMC 9780141394534

KOŁAKOWSKI, LESZEK
Is God Happy? Selected Essays
    trans. by Agnieszka Kołakowska
    PMC 9780141389554

KOMNENE, ANNA
The Alexiad
    trans. by E. R. A. Sewter, rev. Peter Frankopan
    PC 9780140455274

The Koran
>trans. by N. J. Dawood
>PC 9780141393834
>trans. by N. J. Dawood (with Parallel Arabic Text)
>PC 9780141393841
>trans. by Tarif Khalidi (as *The Qur'an*)
>PC 9780140455441; Deluxe 9780143105886

KPOMASSIE, TÉTÉ-MICHEL
Michel the Giant: An African in Greenland
>trans. by James Kirkup & Ros Schwartz
>PMC 9780241554531

KRAF, ELAINE
I Am Clarence
>PMC 9780241766859
The Princess of 72nd Street
>PMC 9780241715277

KROPOTKIN, PETER
Anarchist Communism
>Great Ideas 9780241472408
The Conquest of Bread
>PC 9780141396118
Mutual Aid
>PC 9780241355336

KRÚDY, GYULA
 Life Is a Dream
  trans. by John Batki
  PMC 9780141193038

L

LA FONTAINE, JEAN DE
Selected Fables
    trans. by James Michie
    PC 9780140455243
The World is Full of Foolish Men
    trans. by James Michie
    LBC 9780241250402

LA ROCHEFOUCAULD, FRANÇOIS DE
Maxims
    trans. by Leonard Tancock
    PC 9780140440959

LACLOS, CHODERLOS DE
Dangerous Liaisons
    trans. by Helen Constantine
    PC 9780140449570

LAFAYETTE, MADAME DE
The Princesse de Clèves
    trans. by Robin Buss
    PC 9780140445879

LAGERLÖF, SELMA
A Book for Christmas
    trans. by Peter Graves, Sarah Death & Linda Schenck
    HB 9780241715062
The Wonderful Adventure of Nils Holgersson
    trans. by Paul Norlen
    PC 9780241206096

LAING, KOJO
Search Sweet Country
    PMC 9780241370094

LAING, R. D.
The Divided Self
    PMC 9780141189376

LAMB, CHARLES
Selected Prose
    PC 9780141392912
Tales from Shakespeare
with Mary Lamb
    PC 9780141441627

LAMMING, GEORGE
In the Castle of My Skin
    PMC 9780241296066

LANGEWIESCHE, WILLIAM
Aloft
PMC 9780141191850

LANGLAND, WILLIAM
Piers the Ploughman
trans. by J. F. Goodridge
PC 9780140440874

LANYER, AEMILIA
with Mary Sidney & Isabella Whitney
Renaissance Women Poets
PC 9780140424096

LAO SHE
Mr Ma and Son
trans. by William Dolby
PMC 9780241579558

LAO TZU
Tao Te Ching
trans. by D. C. Lau
PC 9780140441314; Great Ideas 9780141043685
trans. by John Minford
Deluxe 9780143133803

LARSEN, NELLA
> *Passing*
>> PC 9780142437278; PEL 9780241472712;
>> LCC 9780241573747
>
> *Quicksand*
>> PEL 9780241652657

LARTÉGUY, JEAN
> *The Centurions*
>> trans. by Xan Fielding
>> PC 9780143107446
>
> *The Praetorians*
>> trans. by Xan Fielding
>> PC 9780143110231

LAS CASAS, BARTOLOMÉ DE
> *A Short Account of the Destruction of the Indies*
>> trans. by Nigel Griffin
>> PC 9780140445626

Latin Literature: An Anthology
> ed. by Michael Grant
> PC 9780141398112

LAUTRÉAMONT, COMTE DE
> *Maldoror* and *Poems*
>> trans. by Paul Knight
>> PC 9780140443424

LAWRENCE, D. H.

Apocalypse
PMC 9780140187816

D. H. Lawrence and Italy
PC 9780141441559

The Fox, The Captain's Doll, The Ladybird
PC 9780141441832

Lady Chatterley's Lover
PC 9780141441498; Clothbound 9780141192482

Life with a Capital L: Essays
Design 9780241344606

Odour of Chrysanthemum
Archive 9780241746974

The Prussian Officer and Other Stories
PMC 9780140187809

The Rainbow
PC 9780141441382

Sea and Sardinia
PMC 9780141180762

Selected Poems
PC 9780140424584

Selected Stories
PC 9780141441658

Sons and Lovers
PC 9780141441443; PEL 9780141199856

Studies in Classic American Literature
    PMC 9780140183771
The Woman Who Rode Away, St. Mawr, The Princess
    PC 9780141441665
Women in Love
    PC 9780141441542

LAWRENCE, T. E.
Seven Pillars of Wisdom
    PMC 9780141182766

The Laws of Manu
    trans. by Wendy Doniger & Brian K. Smith
    PC 9780140445404

Lazarillo de Tormes and The Swindler: Two Spanish Picaresque Novels
    trans. by Michael Alpert
    PC 9780140449006

LE CARRÉ, JOHN
Absolute Friends
    PMC 9780241321935
Call for the Dead
    PMC 9780141198286; HB 9780241521809;
    Crime 9780241639214
The Constant Gardener
    PMC 9780241322307

A Delicate Truth
   HB 9780241396360
The Honourable Schoolboy
   PMC 9780241322352; NS 9780241330906
A Legacy of Spies
   HB 9780241396384
The Little Drummer Girl
   PMC 9780241322376
The Looking Glass War
   PMC 9780141196398
The Mission Song
   PMC 9780241322390; HB 9780241337271
A Most Wanted Man
   PMC 9780241322420; HB 9780241337288
A Murder of Quality
   PMC 9780141196374; HB 9780241337127
The Naive and Sentimental Lover
   PMC 9780241322444; HB 9780241337295
The Night Manager
   PMC 9780141393018; Crime 9780241685051
Our Game
   PMC 9780241243619; HB 9780241337226
Our Kind of Traitor
   HB 9780241396353
A Perfect Spy
   PMC 9780241322482

The Pigeon Tunnel: Stories from My Life
    HB 9780241396377
The Russia House
    PMC 9780141196350
The Secret Pilgrim
    PMC 9780141196367
Single & Single
    PMC 9780241322505; HB 9780241337318
A Small Town in Germany
    PMC 9780141196381; HB 9780241337196
Smiley's People
    PMC 9780241322529
The Spy Who Came in from the Cold
    PMC 9780141194523; HB 9780241771037
The Tailor of Panama
    PMC 9780241291733
Tinker Tailor Soldier Spy
    PMC 9780241323410; Clothbound 9780241685143; Crime 9780241658987

LE CLÉZIO, J. M. G.
Fever
    trans. by Daphne Woodward
    PMC 9780141191423
The Flood
    trans. by Peter Green
    PMC 9780141191409

Terra Amata
    trans. by Barbara Bray
    PMC 9780141191416

LE FANU, J. S.
Uncle Silas
    PC 9780140437461

LEAR, EDWARD
The Complete Nonsense and Other Verse
    PC 9780140424652

LEARY, TIMOTHY
with Richard Alpert & Ralph Metzner
The Psychedelic Experience
    PMC 9780141189635

LEBLANC, MAURICE
Arsène Lupin, Gentleman-Thief
    trans. by Michael Sims
    PC 9780143104865
The Escape of Arsène Lupin
    trans. by Michael Sims
    Archive 9780241752319

LEE, LAURIE
As I Walked Out One Midsummer Morning
    PMC 9780241953280

Collected Poems
    PMC 9780241625187; HB 9780241625170
Down in the Valley: A Writer's Landscape
    PMC 9780241411698
I Can't Stay Long
    PMC 9780241237175
A Moment of War
    PMC 9780241953297; Archive 9780241752043
Village Christmas and Other Notes on the English Year
    PMC 9780241243671

LEE, STAN
  The Amazing Spider-Man
  with Steve Ditko
    Marvel 9780143135739
  The Avengers
  with Jack Kirby, Roy Thomas, Don Heck, John Buscema & Sal Buscema
    Marvel 9780143135791; Marvel HB 9780143135784
  Black Panther
  with Don McGregor, Rich Buckler, Billy Graham & Jack Kirby
    Marvel 9780143135814; Marvel HB 9780143135807
  Captain America
  with Joe Simon, Jack Kirby, Jim Steranko & John Romita Sr.
    Marvel 9780143135753; Marvel HB 9780143135746

Fantastic Four
with Jack Kirby
   Marvel 9780143135838; Marvel HB 9780143135821
X-Men
with Jack Kirby, Roy Thomas, Werner Roth, Don Heck & Neal Adams
   Marvel 9780143135777; Marvel HB 9780143135760

LEM, Stanisław
The Cyberiad
   trans. by Michael Kandel
   PMC 9780141394596; Sci-Fi 9780241467992
Fiasco
   trans. by Michael Kandel
   PMC 9780241334355
The Futurological Congress
   trans. by Michael Kandel
   PMC 9780241312780
Mortal Engines
   trans. by Michael Kandel
   PMC 9780241269077
The Seventh Voyage
   trans. by Michael Kandel & Louis Iribarne
   Archive 9780241752265
The Star Diaries
   trans. by Michael Kandel
   PMC 9780241240021

Tales of Pirx the Pilot
    trans. by Louis Iribarne
    PMC 9780241400227
The Three Electroknights
    trans. by Michael Kandel
    PM 9780241339398

LENIN, VLADIMIR
Imperialism: The Highest Stage of Capitalism
    Great Ideas 9780141192567
The State and Revolution
    trans. by Robert Service
    PC 9780140184358

LENNOX, CHARLOTTE
The Female Quixote
    PC 9780140439878

LEO AFRICANUS, JOHANNES
(Al-Hasan Ibn Muhammad Al-Wazzan)
The Cosmography and Geography of Africa
    trans. by Anthony Ossa-Richardson & Richard Oosterhoff
    PC 9780241543931

LEONARD, ELMORE
52 Pickup
    Crime 9780241755327

Cat Chaser
   Crime 9780241755310
City Primeval
   Crime 9780241755334
Glitz
   Crime 9780241755341
Hombre and *Three-Ten to Yuma*
   Westerns 9780241755358
The Hunted
   Crime 9780241755365
Last Stand at Saber River
   Westerns 9780241755389
Picket Line and Other Stories
   Crime 9780241755396
Rum Punch
   Crime 9780241755402
Swag
   Crime 9780241755419
The Switch
   Crime 9780241755426
Unknown Man No. 89
   Crime 9780241755433
Valdez is Coming
   Westerns 9780241755440

LEOPARDI, GIACOMO
Canti
trans. by Jonathan Galassi
PC 9780141193878

LEOPOLD, ALDO
A Sand County Almanac and Sketches Here and There
PC 9780241402993
Think Like a Mountain
Green 9780241514665

LERMONTOV, MIKHAIL
A Hero of Our Time
trans. by Natasha Randall
PC 9780143105633

LERNET-HOLENIA, ALEXANDER
Baron Bagge
trans. by Richard Winston & Clara Winston
PMC 9780241615621; Archive 9780241752449
Count Luna
trans. by Jane B. Greene
PMC 9780241649541
Mars in Aries
trans. by Robert Dassanowsky & John Barrett
PMC 9780241674468

LEROUX, GASTON
- *The Phantom of the Opera*
  - trans. by Mireille Ribière
  - PC 9780141191508; Clothbound 9780241725429

LESKOV, NIKOLAI
- *Lady Macbeth of Mtsensk and Other Stories*
  - trans. by David McDuff
  - PC 9780141396743
- *Night Owls*
  - trans. by Hugh McLean
  - Archive 9780241752197

LEVI, CARLO
- *Christ Stopped at Eboli*
  - trans. by Frances Frenaye
  - PMC 9780141183213

LEVI, PRIMO
- *If Not Now, When?*
  - trans. by William Weaver
  - PMC 9780141183909
- *Moments of Reprieve*
  - trans. by Ruth Feldman
  - PMC 9780141186979
- *The Periodic Table*
  - trans. by Raymond Rosenthal
  - PMC 9780141185149

A Tranquil Star
    trans. by Ann Goldstein & Alessandra Bastagli
    PMC 9780141188911

LÉVI-STRAUSS, CLAUDE
Tristes Tropiques
    trans. by John & Doreen Weightman
    PMC 9780141197548

LEWIS, MATTHEW
The Monk
    PC 9780140436037

LEWIS, SINCLAIR
It Can't Happen Here
    PMC 9780241310663

LEWIS, WYNDHAM
The Revenge for Love
    PMC 9780141187648
The Wild Body
    PMC 9780141187631

LI PO
with Tu Fu
Poems
    trans. by Arthur Cooper
    PC 9780140442724

LI QINGZHAO
- *The Magpie at Night*
    - trans. by Wendy Chen
    - Demy 9780241774076

LIANG QICHAO
- *Thoughts From the Ice-Drinker's Studio: Essays on China and the World*
    - trans. by Peter Zarrow
    - PC 9780241568781

LIEBLING, A. J.
- *Between Meals: An Appetite for Paris*
    - PMC 9780241637975
- *The Sweet Science: Boxing and Boxiana – A Ringside View*
    - PMC 9780241343203

LIGOTTI, THOMAS
- *Songs of a Dead Dreamer* and *Grimscribe*
    - PC 9780143107767

LINDSAY, DAVID
- *A Voyage to Arcturus*
    - Sci-Fi 9780241441589

LINNA, VÄINÖ
- *Unknown Soldiers*
    - trans. by Liesl Yamaguchi
    - PMC 9780141393650

LISPECTOR, CLARICE

Água Viva
trans. by Stefan Tobler
PMC 9780141197364

The Apple in the Dark
trans. by Benjamin Moser
PMC 9780241371350

An Apprenticeship or The Book of Pleasures
trans. by Stefan Tobler
PMC 9780241371367

The Besieged City
trans. by Johnny Lorenz
PMC 9780241371374

A Breath of Life
trans. by Johnny Lorenz
PMC 9780141197371

The Burned Sinner and the Harmonious Angels
trans. by Katrina Dodson
Archive 9780241752357

The Chandelier
trans. by Benjamin Moser & Magdalena Edwards
PMC 9780241371343

Complete Stories
trans. by Katrina Dodson
PMC 9780141197388

Daydream and Drunkenness of a Young Lady
trans. by Katrina Dodson
PM 9780241337608

Hour of the Star
    trans. by Benjamin Moser
    PMC 9780141392035
The Imitation of the Rose
    trans. by Katrina Dodson
    LCC 9780241630846
Near to the Wild Heart
    trans. by Alison Entrekin
    PMC 9780141197340
The Passion According to G. H.
    trans. by Idra Novey
    PMC 9780141197357
Too Much of Life
    trans. by Margaret Jull Costa & Robin Patterson
    PMC 9780241597583

LITVINOFF, EMANUEL
Journey Through a Small Planet
    PMC 9780141189307

LIVELY, PENELOPE
According to Mark
    PMC 9780141196831
Heat Wave
    PMC 9780141196824
Moon Tiger
    PMC 9780141188317

Oleander, Jacaranda
    PMC 9780141188324

Lives of Roman Christian Women
    trans. by Carolinne White
    PC 9780141441931

Lives of the Later Caesars
    trans. by Anthony Birley
    PC 9780140443080

LIVY
    The History of Rome from its Foundation
        The Early History of Rome: Books 1–5
        trans. by Aubrey de Sélincourt
        PC 9780140448092
        Rome and Italy: Books 6–10
        trans. by Betty Radice
        PC 9780140443882
        The War with Hannibal: Books 21–30
        trans. by Aubrey de Sélincourt
        PC 9780140441451
        Rome and the Mediterranean: Books 31–45
        trans. by Henry Bettenson
        PC 9780140443189

LLEWELLYN, RICHARD
    How Green Was My Valley
        PMC 9780141185859

LOCHTE, DICK
  Sleeping Dog
    Crime 9780241656921

LOCKE, JOHN
  An Essay Concerning Human Understanding
    PC 9780140434828
  On the Abuse of Words
    Great Ideas 9780141043876

LONDON, JACK
  The Call of the Wild
    PEL 9780241341490
  The Call of the Wild, White Fang and Other Stories
    PC 9780140186512
  Martin Eden
    PC 9780140187724
  Tales of the Pacific
    PMC 9780140183580
  White Fang
    PEL 9780241652664

LONGUS
  Daphnis and Chloe
    trans. by Paul Turner
    PC 9780140440591
  see also *Greek Fiction*

LOOS, ADOLF
: *Ornament and Crime*
: Design 9780141392974

LORCA, FEDERICO GARCÍA
: *Cicada!*
: trans. by Catherine Brown, Alan S. Trueblood & Tyler Fisher
: Archive 9780241746844
: *Gypsy Ballads*
: trans. by Tyler Fisher
: PC 9780241371879
: *The House of Bernarda Alba and Other Plays*
: trans. by Michael Dewell & Carmen Zapata
: PMC 9780141185750
: *Poet in New York*
: trans. by Greg Simon & Steven F. White
: PMC 9780141185828
: *Selected Poems*
: ed. by Christopher Maurer
: PMC 9780141185835

LORDE, AUDRE
: *The Black Unicorn*
: PMC 9780241396865
: *The Cancer Journals*
: PMC 9780241453506

Coal
   Archive 9780241752418
The Master's Tools Will Never Dismantle the Master's House
   PM 9780241339725
Sister Outsider
   PMC 9780241410509
When I Dare to Be Powerful
   Great Ideas 9780241473153
Zami: A New Spelling of my Name
   PMC 9780241351086

LOTT, TIM
   The Scent of Dried Roses
      PMC 9780141191485

LOVECRAFT, H. P.
   At the Mountains of Madness
      PEL 9780241341315
   The Call of Cthulhu and Other Weird Stories
      PC 9780141182346; Deluxe 9780143106487
   The Colour Out of Space
      Sci-Fi 9780241443934
   The Dreams in the Witch House and Other Weird Stories
      PC 9780142437957
   The Dunwich Horror and Other Stories
      NS 9780141038766

The Shadow out of Time
  Archive 9780241746837
The Thing on the Doorstep and Other Weird Stories
  PC 9780142180037; HB 9780143122326

LOVELOCK, JAMES
We Belong to Gaia
  Green 9780241514641

LOWRY, MALCOLM
Under the Volcano
  PMC 9780141182254

LU XUN
The Real Story of Ah-Q and Other Tales of China: The Complete Fiction of Lu Xun
  trans. by Julia Lovell
  PC 9780140455489

LUCIAN
Chattering Courtesans and Other Sardonic Sketches
  trans. by Keith Sidwell
  PC 9780140447026

LUCRETIUS
The Nature of Things
  trans. by A. E. Stallings
  PC 9780140447965; Pocket HB 9780141396903

LUO GUANZHONG
The Romance of the Three Kingdoms
trans. by Martin Palmer, He Yun, Jay Ramsay & Victoria Finlay
PC 9780241332771

LUTHER, MARTIN
The Ninety-Five Theses and Other Writings
trans. by William Russell
PC 9780143107583

LYELL, CHARLES
Principles of Geology
PC 9780140435283

M

MAATHAI, WANGARI
The World We Once Lived In
Green 9780141996936

The Mabinogion
trans. by Jeffrey Gantz
PC 9780140443226

MACAULAY, THOMAS
The History of England
PC 9780140431339

MACDONALD, GEORGE
The Complete Fairy Tales
PC 9780140437379

MACDONALD, ROSS
The Chill
PMC 9780141196619
The Drowning Pool
PMC 9780141196626; Crime 9780241639191

The Galton Case
    PMC 9780141196633
The Goodbye Look
    PMC 9780141196602
The Underground Man
    PMC 9780141196589; Crime 9780241684795

MACHADO DE ASSIS
The Posthumous Memoirs of Brás Cubas
    trans. by Flora Thomson-DeVeaux
    PC 9780143135036

MACHEN, ARTHUR
The Great God Pan
    PEL 9780241341124
The White People and Other Weird Stories
    PC 9780143105596

MACHIAVELLI, NICCOLÒ
The Discourses
    trans. by Leslie J. Walter, rev. Brian Richardson
    PC 9780140444285
On Conspiracies
    trans. by Leslie J. Walter, rev. Brian Richardson
    Great Ideas 9780141192772

The Prince
    trans. by George Bull
    Great Ideas 9780141018850
    trans. by Tim Parks
    PC 9780141442259; Pocket HB 9780141395876

MACLAREN-ROSS, JULIAN
Of Love and Hunger
    PMC 9780141187112

MACLAVERTY, BERNARD
Cal
    Student 9780140817898

MADISON, JAMES
with Alexander Hamilton & John Jay
The Federalist Papers
    PC 9780140444957

Magna Carta
    trans. by David Carpenter
    PC 9780241953372

The Mahabharata
    trans. R. K. Narayan
    PMC 9780141185002
    trans. by John D. Smith
    PC 9780140446814

MAI JIA
- *Decoded: A Novel*
  - trans. by Olivia Milburn & Christopher N. Payne
  - NS 9780141391489

MAILER, NORMAN
- *Advertisements for Myself*
  - PMC 9780241340455
- *An American Dream*
  - PMC 9780241340516
- *The Armies of the Night: History as a Novel / The Novel as History*
  - PMC 9780241340479
- *The Fight*
  - PMC 9780141184142
- *A Fire on the Moon*
  - PMC 9780141394961
- *Miami and the Siege of Chicago: An Informal History of the Republican and Democratic Conventions of 1968*
  - PMC 9780241340530
- *Mind of an Outlaw: Selected Essays*
  - PMC 9780141394985
- *The Naked and the Dead*
  - PMC 9780241340493

MAJOR, CLARENCE
Dirty Bird Blues
PC 9780143136590

MALCOLM X
with Alex Haley
The Autobiography of Malcolm X
PMC 9780141185439

MALORY, THOMAS
Le Morte D'Arthur
Volume 1
PC 9780140430431
Volume 2
PC 9780140430448
retold by Peter Ackroyd (as *The Death of King Arthur*)
PC 9780140455656

MALRAUX, ANDRÉ
Man's Fate
trans. by Haskon M. Chevalier
PMC 9780141190983

MALTHUS, THOMAS
An Essay on the Principle of Population and Other Writings
PC 9780141392820

MANDELA, NELSON
No Easy Walk to Freedom: Speeches, Letters and Other Writings
PMC 9780141439303

MANDEVILLE, BERNARD
The Fable of the Bees
PC 9780140445411

MANDEVILLE, SIR JOHN
The Travels of Sir John Mandeville
trans. by C. W. R. D. Moseley
PC 9780141441436

MANN, SALLY
Hold Still
Design 9780241699287

MANNING, FREDERIC
The Middle Parts of Fortune: Somme and Ancre, 1916
PMC 9780141393414

MANSFIELD, KATHERINE
Bliss
LCC 9780241619797
The Collected Stories of Katherine Mansfield
PC 9780141441818

A Dill Pickle
    Archive 9780241746752
The Garden Party
    PEL 9780241341643
The Garden Party and Other Stories
    PC 9780141441801

MANTO, SAADAT HASAN
The Price of Freedom
    trans. by Khalid Hasan
    Archive 9780241747223

MANZONI, ALESSANDRO
The Betrothed
    trans. by Bruce Penman
    PC 9780140442748

MARCELLINUS, AMMIANUS
The Later Roman Empire (A.D. 354–378)
    trans. by Walter Hamilton
    PC 9780140444063

MARECHERA, DAMBUDZO
The House of Hunger
    PMC 9780241544259; Archive 9780241752241

MARGUERITE DE NAVARRE
: *The Heptameron*
    trans. by P. A. Chilton
    PC 9780140443554

MARÍAS, JAVIER
: *All Souls*
    trans. by Margaret Jull Costa
    PMC 9780141389240
: *Dark Back of Time*
    trans. by Esther Allen
    PMC 9780141199894
: *A Heart So White*
    trans. by Margaret Jull Costa
    PMC 9780141199955
: *Madame du Deffand and the Idiots*
    trans. by Margaret Jull Costa
    PM 9780241339480
: *The Man of Feeling*
    trans. by Margaret Jull Costa
    PMC 9780141389257
: *Tomorrow in the Battle Think on Me*
    trans. by Margaret Jull Costa
    PMC 9780141199986
: *When I Was Mortal*
    trans. by Margaret Jull Costa
    PMC 9780141389264

Written Lives
    trans. by Margaret Jull Costa
    PMC 9780141389271
Your Face Tomorrow
    trans. by Margaret Jull Costa
    Volume 1: Fever and Spear
    PMC 9780241288894
    Volume 2: Dance and Dream
    PMC 9780241288917
    Volume 3: Poison, Shadow and Farewell
    PMC 9780241338063

MARIE DE FRANCE
The Lais of Marie De France
    trans. by Glyn S. Burgess & Keith Busby
    PC 9780140447590

MARINETTI, FILIPPO TOMMASO
The Futurist Cookbook
    trans. by Suzanne Brill
    PMC 9780141391649

MARLOWE, CHRISTOPHER
The Complete Plays
    PC 9780140436334

MÁRQUEZ, GABRIEL GARCÍA
Love in the Time of Cholera
trans. by Edith Grossman
PMC 9780141189208
One Hundred Years of Solitude
trans. by Gregory Rabassa
PMC 9780141184999

MARSH, RICHARD
The Beetle
PEL 9780241341353

MARTIAL
The Epigrams
trans. by James Mitchie
PC 9780140443509

MARVELL, ANDREW
The Complete Poems
PC 9780140424577

MARX, GROUCHO
The Essential Groucho
ed. by Stefan Kanfer
PMC 9780141189444

MARX, KARL
- *Capital*
  - *Volume I*
  - trans. by Ben Fowkes
  - PC 9780140445688
  - *Volume II*
  - trans. by David Fernbach
  - PC 9780140445695
  - *Volume III*
  - trans. by David Fernbach
  - PC 9780140445701
- *The Communist Manifesto*
- with Friedrich Engels
  - trans. by Samuel Moore
  - PC 9780140447576; Pocket HB 9780141395906; Great Ideas 9780141018935; LBC 9780141397986
- *Dispatches for the* New York Tribune*: Selected Journalism*
  - ed. by James Ledbetter
  - PC 9780141441924
- *Early Writings*
  - trans. by Rodney Livingstone & Gregor Benton
  - PC 9780140445749
- *Grundrisse*
  - trans. by Martin Nicolaus
  - PC 9780140445756

MASTUR, KHADIJA
The Women's Courtyard
    trans. by Daisy Rockwell
    PC 9780143138068

MATHESON, RICHARD
The Best of Richard Matheson
    PC 9780143130178

MATSUMOTO, SEICHŌ
Inspector Imanishi Investigates
    trans. by Beth Cary
    PMC 9780241724439
A Quiet Place
    trans. by Louise Heal Kawai
    PMC 9780241744208
Suspicion
    trans. by Jesse Kirkwood
    PMC 9780241724422; NS 9780241756409
Tokyo Express
    trans. by Jesse Kirkwood
    PMC 9780241439081

MATURIN, CHARLES
Melmoth the Wanderer
    PC 9780140447613; PEL 9780241366547

MATUTE, ANA MARÍA
> *The Island*
>> trans. by Laura Lonsdale
>> PMC 9780241374283

MAUPASSANT, GUY DE
> *Bel-Ami*
>> trans. by Douglas Parmée
>> PC 9780140443158
>
> *Femme Fatale*
>> trans. by Siân Miles
>> LBC 9780141398334
>
> *Moonlight*
>> trans. by Siân Miles
>> LCC 9780241619803
>
> *A Parisian Affair and Other Stories*
>> trans. by Siân Miles
>> PC 9780140448122
>
> *Pierre and Jean*
>> trans. by Leonard Tancock
>> PC 9780140443585

MAURIAC, FRANÇOIS
> *Thérèse*
>> (*Thérèse Desqueyroux, Thérèse chez le docteur, Thérèse à l'hôtel, La Fin de la nuit*)
>> trans. by Gerard Hopkins
>> PMC 9780141186221

Thérèse Desqueyroux
   trans. by Gerard Hopkins
   PMC 9780141394053

MAYHEW, HENRY
  London Labour and the London Poor
   PC 9780140432411

MCCULLERS, CARSON
  The Ballad of the Sad Café
   PMC 9780141183695; LCC 9780241590546
  Clock Without Hands
   PMC 9780140083583
  The Haunted Boy
   PM 9780241339503
  The Heart is a Lonely Hunter
   PMC 9780141185224
  The Member of the Wedding
   PMC 9780141182827
  The Mortgaged Heart
   PMC 9780140081954
  Reflections in a Golden Eye
   PMC 9780141184456; Archive 9780241752029

MCGOUGH, ROGER
  with Adrian Henri & Brian Patten
  The Mersey Sound
   PMC 9780141189260

MCGREGOR, DON
   with Rich Buckler, Billy Graham, Stan Lee & Jack Kirby
   Black Panther
      Marvel 9780143135814; Marvel HB 9780143135807

MCKAY, CLAUDE
   Home to Harlem
      PC 9780143138587
   Romance in Marseille
      PC 9780143134220

MCKIBBEN, BILL
   The End of Nature
      PMC 9780241514429
   An Idea Can Go Extinct
      Green 9780241514412

MCLUHAN, MARSHALL
   with Quentin Fiore
   The Medium is the Massage
      Design 9780141035826

MCMURTRY, LARRY
   The Last Picture Show
      PMC 9780141194448

Medieval English Verse
> trans. by Brian Stone
> PC 9780140441444

Medieval Writings on Secular Women
> trans. by Patricia Skinner & Elizabeth van Houts
> PC 9780141439914

MELVILLE, HERMAN
Billy Budd, Bartleby and Other Stories
> PC 9780143107606

The Confidence-Man
> PC 9780140445473

Moby-Dick, or, The Whale
> PC 9780142437247; Clothbound 9780141199603;
> PEL 9780141198958; Deluxe 9780143105954

Redburn
> PC 9780140431056

MENANDER
Plays and Fragments
> trans. by Norma Miller
> PC 9780140445015
> see also *Classical Comedy*

Mencius
> trans. by D. C. Lau
> PC 9780140449716

MEREDITH, GEORGE
The Egoist
PC 9780140430349

Metaphysical Poetry
ed. by Colin Burrow
PC 9780140424447

METZNER, RALPH
with Timothy Leary & Richard Alpert
The Psychedelic Experience
PMC 9780141189635

MICHELANGELO
Selected Poems and Letters
trans. by Anthony Mortimer
PC 9780140449563

MIDDLETON, THOMAS
Five Plays
(*A Trick to Catch the Old One*, *The Revenger's Tragedy*, *A Chaste Maid in Cheapside*, *Women Beware Women*, *The Changeling*)
PC 9780140432190
see also *Three Revenge Tragedies* and *Five Revenge Tragedies*

MILL, JOHN STUART
Autobiography
PC 9780140433166
On Liberty
PC 9780140432077; Great Ideas 9780141046945
On Liberty and *The Subjection of Women*
PC 9780141441474
Utilitarianism and Other Essays
PC 9780140432725

MILLER, ARTHUR
After the Fall
PMC 9780141189994
All My Sons
PMC 9780141189970
The Crucible
PMC 9780141182551
Death of a Salesman
PMC 9780141182742
An Enemy of the People: An Adaptation of the Play by Henrik Ibsen
PMC 9780241198865
Focus
PMC 9780141190044
Incident at Vichy
PMC 9780141190020

The Price
   PMC 9780141189987
Resurrection Blues
   PMC 9780241198926
The Ride Down Mt. Morgan
   PMC 9780241198889
A View from the Bridge
   PMC 9780141189963

MILLER, HENRY
Aller Retour New York
   PMC 9780141398860
The Colossus of Maroussi
   PMC 9780141980546
Nexus
   PMC 9780141399102
Plexus
   PMC 9780141399126
Quiet Days in Clichy
   PMC 9780141399164
Sexus
   PMC 9780141399119
Tropic of Cancer
   PMC 9780141399133
Tropic of Capricorn
   PMC 9780141399140

The World of Sex
　NS 9780141399157

MILLER, MERLE
　On Being Different: What It Means to Be a Homosexual
　PC 9780143106968

MIŁOSZ, CZESŁAW
　The Captive Mind
　　trans. by Jane Zielonko
　　PMC 9780141186764
　Native Realm: A Search for Self-Definition
　　trans. by Catherine S. Leach
　　PMC 9780141392288
　New and Collected Poems 1931–2001
　　trans. by Czesław Miłosz, Robert Hass et al.
　　PMC 9780141186412
　Proud To Be a Mammal
　　trans. by Catherine S. Leach, Bogdana Carpenter
　　& Madeline G. Levine
　　PMC 9780141193199
　Rescue
　　trans. by Czesław Miłosz, Robert Hass et al.
　　Archive 9780241752395
　Selected and Last Poems 1931–2004
　　ed. by Robert Hass and Anthony Miłosz
　　PMC 9780141392301

MILTON, JOHN
Areopagitica and Other Writings
PC 9780140439069
The Complete Poems
PC 9780140433630
Paradise Lost
PC 9780140424393; Clothbound 9780141394633
Selected Poems
PC 9780140424416

Minor Notes, Volume 1
ed. by Joshua Bennett & Jesse McCarthy
PC 9780143137269

The Mirror of My Heart: A Thousand Years of Persian Poetry by Women
trans. by Dick Davis
PC 9780143135616

MISHIMA, YUKIO
Beautiful Star
trans. by Stephen Dodd
PMC 9780241441091
Confessions of a Mask
trans. by Meredith Weatherby
PMC 9780241301197

Death in Midsummer
   trans. by Edward G. Seidensticker, Donald Keene, Geoffrey W. Sargent & Ivan Morris
   PMC 9780241678947; LCC 9780241630853
Forbidden Colours
   trans. by Alfred H. Marks
   PMC 9780141189567
The Frolic of the Beasts
   trans. by Andrew Clare
   PMC 9780241386705; NS 9780241675311
Life for Sale
   trans. by Stephen Dodd
   PMC 9780241333150
Star
   trans. by Jonathan Samuel Bett
   PM 9780241383476
Voices of the Fallen Heroes and Other Stories
   ed. by Stephen Dodd
   PMC 9780241723616

MITFORD, NANCY
The Letters of Nancy Mitford and Evelyn Waugh
with Evelyn Waugh
   PMC 9780141193922

The Pursuit of Love and Other Novels
  (*Love in a Cold Climate*, *The Pursuit of Love*, *The Blessing*)
  PMC 9780241514993

MO ZI
  The Book of Master Mo
   trans. by Ian Johnston
   PC 9780141392103

MODIANO, PATRICK
  Missing Person
   trans. by Daniel Weissbort
   PMC 9780241402184

MOLIÈRE
  The Misanthrope and Other Plays
   trans. by John Wood, rev. David Coward
   PC 9780140447309
  The Miser and Other Plays
   trans. by John Wood, rev. David Coward
   PC 9780140447286
  see also *Four French Plays*

MONBIOT, GEORGE
  This Can't Be Happening
   Green 9780241514634

MONTAGU, MARY WORTLEY
Selected Letters
PC 9780140434903

MONTAIGNE, MICHEL DE
An Apology for Raymond Sebond
trans. by M. A. Screech
PC 9780140444933
Essays
trans. by J. M. Cohen
NS 9780140178975
The Essays: A Selection
trans. by M. A. Screech
PC 9780140446029
The Complete Essays
trans. by M. A. Screech
PC 9780140446043
On Friendship
trans. by M. A. Screech
Great Ideas 9780141018867
On Solitude
trans. by M. A. Screech
Great Ideas 9780141043852

MONTESQUIEU, BARON
Persian Letters
trans. by Christopher Betts
PC 9780140442816

MONTGOMERY, L. M.
Anne of Green Gables
Deluxe 9780143131854

MORANTE, ELSA
Lies and Sorcery
trans. by Jenny McPhee
PMC 9780241711200; Demy 9780241711194

MORE, THOMAS
Utopia
trans. by Paul Turner
Great Ideas 9780141043692
trans. by Dominic Baker-Smith
PC 9780141442327; Pocket HB 9780241382684

MÖRIKE, EDUARD
Mozart's Journey to Prague and Selected Poems
trans. by David Luke
PC 9780140447378

MORRIS, WILLIAM
News from Nowhere and Other Writings
PC 9780140433302
Useful Work versus Useless Toil
Great Ideas 9780141036700

MORRISSEY
Autobiography
PMC 9780141394817

MORTIMER, JOHN
  Clinging to the Wreckage
    PMC 9780141193847
  The Collected Stories of Rumpole
    PMC 9780141198293
  Paradise Postponed
    PMC 9780141193397
  Rumpole of the Bailey
    PMC 9780241398883
  Rumpole's Return
    PMC 9780241474440
  The Trials of Rumpole
    PMC 9780241474433

MORTIMER, PENELOPE
  The Pumpkin Eater
    PMC 9780241240106

MORTON, TIMOTHY
  All Art is Ecological
    Green 9780141997001

MOZART, WOLFGANG AMADEUS
  A Life in Letters
    trans. by Stewart Spencer
    PC 9780141441467

MROŻEK, SŁAWOMIR
- *The Elephant*
  - trans. by Konrad Syrop
  - PMC 9780141193045

MULTATULI
- *Max Havelaar*
  - trans. by Roy Edwards
  - PC 9780140445169

MUNARI, BRUNO
- *Design as Art*
  - trans. by Patrick Creagh
  - Design 9780141035819

MURASAKI SHIKIBU, LADY
- *The Diary of Lady Murasaki*
  - trans. by Richard Bowring
  - PC 9780140435764
- *The Tale of Genji*
  - trans. by Royall Tyler
  - Deluxe 9780142437148

MUSSET, ALFRED DE
- *The Confession of a Child of the Century*
  - trans. by David Coward
  - PC 9780141391854

NABOKOV, VLADIMIR
Ada or Ardor
PMC 9780141181875
Bend Sinister
PMC 9780141185767
Collected Poems
trans. by Dmitri Nabokov
PMC 9780141192260
Collected Stories
trans. by Dmitri Nabokov
PMC 9780141183459
The Defense
trans. by Michael Scammell & Vladimir Nabokov
PMC 9780241720486
Despair
trans. by Vladimir Nabokov
PMC 9780141184548
The Enchanter
trans. by Dmitri Nabokov
PMC 9780141191188

The Eye
 trans. by Dmitri Nabokov & Vladimir Nabokov
 PMC 9780140184822

The Gift
 trans. by Michael Scammell, Dmitri Nabokov & Vladimir Nabokov
 PMC 9780141185873

Glory
 trans. by Dmitri Nabokov & Vladimir Nabokov
 PMC 9780141188515

Invitation to a Beheading
 trans. by Dmitri Nabokov & Vladimir Nabokov
 PMC 9780141185606

King, Queen, Knave
 trans. by Dmitri Nabokov & Vladimir Nabokov
 PMC 9780141185774

Lance
 PM 9780241339527

Laughter in the Dark
 trans. by Vladimir Nabokov
 PMC 9780141186528

Letters to Véra
 trans. by Olga Voronina & Brian Boyd
 PMC 9780141192246

Lolita
 PMC 9780141182537; Clothbound 9780241638439; NS 9780141023496

The Annotated Lolita
   PMC 9780141185040
Look at the Harlequins!
   PMC 9780141198033
Mary
   trans. by Michael Glenny & Vladimir Nabokov
   PMC 9780141191478
Nabokov's Dozen: Thirteen Stories
   trans. by Peter Pertzov & Vladimir Nabokov
   PMC 9780241302484; LCC 9780241630884
Nikolai Gogol
   PMC 9781846143304
The Original of Laura
   PMC 9780141191164
Pale Fire
   PMC 9780141185262
Pnin
   PMC 9780141183756; Clothbound 9780241638422
The Real Life of Sebastian Knight
   PMC 9780141185996
Revenge
   Archive 9780241747001
Speak, Memory: An Autobiography Revisited
   PMC 9780141183220
Think, Write, Speak
   PMC 9780141398389

The Tragedy of Mister Morn
    trans. by Thomas Karshan & Anastasia Tolstoy
   PMC 9780141196329
Transparent Things
   PMC 9780141198040

NÆSS, ARNE
Ecology of Wisdom
   PMC 9780241257197
There is No Point of No Return
   Green 9780241514610

NAFISI, AZAR
Reading Lolita in Tehran
   PMC 9780241246238

NAIPAUL, SHIVA
The Chip-Chip Gatherers
   PMC 9780141197227
Fireflies
   PMC 9780141197234
North of South
   PMC 9780140188264

NAIRN, IAN
Nairn's London
   Design 9780141396156

NARAYAN, R. K.
>*The Guide*
>>PC 9780143039648
>
>*The Mahabharata*
>>PMC 9780141185002
>
>*The Man-Eater of Malgudi*
>>PMC 9780140185485
>
>*The Painter of Signs*
>>PMC 9780140185492
>
>*The Ramayana: A Shortened Modern Prose Version of the Indian Epic*
>>PC 9780143039679
>
>*Under the Banyan Tree and Other Stories*
>>PMC 9780141186214
>
>*The Vendor of Sweets*
>>PMC 9780140185508

NĀRĀYANA
>*The Hitopadeśa*
>>trans. by A. N. D. Haksar
>>PC 9780140455229

NASHE, THOMAS
>*The Unfortunate Traveller and Other Works*
>>PC 9780140430677

NASSAR, RADUAN
Ancient Tillage
trans. by Karen Sotelino
PMC 9780141396781
A Cup of Rage
trans. by Stefan Tobler
PMC 9780141396804

NEDREAAS, TORBORG
Nothing Grows by Moonlight
trans. by Bibbi Lee
Demy 9780241729663

NERVAL, GÉRARD DE
October Nights
trans. by Richard Sieburth
Archive 9780241747247
Selected Writings
trans. by Richard Sieburth
PC 9780140446012

The New Penguin Book of American Short Stories from Washington Irving to Lydia Davis
ed. by Kasia Boddy
PC 9780141194424

The New Penguin Book of English Folk Songs
ed. by Steve Roud & Julia Bishop
PC 9780141194622

NEWMAN, JOHN HENRY
Apologia Pro Vita Sua
PC 9780140433746

NGŨGĨ WA THIONG'O
Devil on the Cross
PC 9780143107361
A Grain of Wheat
PMC 9780141186993
The River Between
PMC 9780141187037

The Nibelungenlied
trans. by A. T. Hatto
PC 9780140441376

NICKERSON, THOMAS
with Owen Chase
The Loss of the Ship Essex *Sunk by a Whale*
PC 9780140437966

NIETZSCHE, FRIEDRICH
Aphorisms on Love and Hate
trans. by Marion Faber & Stephen Lehmann
LBC 9780141397900
Beyond Good and Evil
trans. by R. J. Hollingdale
PC 9780140449235; Pocket HB 9780141395838

The Birth of Tragedy
  trans. by Shaun Whiteside
  PC 9780140433395

Ecce Homo
  trans. by R. J. Hollingdale
  PC 9780140445152; Archive 9780241752227

God is Dead. God Remains Dead. And We Have Killed Him.
  trans. by R. Kevin Hill & Michael A. Scarpitti
  Great Ideas 9780241472842

Human, All Too Human
  trans. by Marion Faber & Stephen Lehmann
  PC 9780140446173

The Joyous Science
  trans. by R. Kevin Hill
  PC 9780141195391

Man Alone with Himself
  trans. by Marion Faber, Stephen Lehmann &
  R. J. Hollingdale
  Great Ideas 9780141036687

A Nietzsche Reader
  trans. by R. J. Hollingdale
  PC 9780140443295

On the Genealogy of Morals
  trans. by Michael A. Scarpitti
  PC 9780141195377

Thus Spoke Zarathustra
    trans. by R. J. Hollingdale
    PC 9780140441185
Twilight of the Idols and The Anti-Christ
    trans. by R. J. Hollingdale
    PC 9780140445145
Why I am So Wise
    trans. by R. J. Hollingdale
    Great Ideas 9780141018973
Why I am So Clever
    LBC 9780241251850
The Will to Power
    trans. by R. Kevin Hill & Michael A. Scarpitti
    PC 9780141195353

NIEVO, IPPOLITO
Confessions of an Italian
    trans. by Frederika Randall
    PC 9780141391663

NIJŌ, LADY
A Tale Unasked
    trans. by Meredith McKinney
    PC 9780241562468

NIN, ANAÏS
Delta of Venus
    PMC 9780141182841

Henry and June
PMC 9780141183282
Little Birds
PMC 9780141183404
A Spy in the House of Love
PMC 9780141183718; LCC 9780241614686
The Veiled Woman
PM 9780241339541

NITOBE, INAZŌ
Bushido: The Soul of Japan
Great Ideas 9780241472439

Njal's Saga
trans. by Robert Cook
PC 9780140447699

NORTHUP, SOLOMON
Twelve Years a Slave
PC 9780143106708

NOSAKA, AKIYUKI
Grave of the Fireflies
trans. by Ginny Tapley Takemori
NS 9780241780213

NOSTRADAMUS
The Prophecies
    trans. by Richard Sieburth
    PC 9780143107231

NOTKER THE STAMMERER
with Einhard
Two Lives of Charlemagne
    trans. by David Ganz
    PC 9780140455052

NYISZLI, MIKLÓS
Auschwitz: A Doctor's Eyewitness Account
    trans. by Tibere Kremer & Richard Sevear
    PMC 9780141392219

O

OBAYD-E ZAKANI
  with Hafez & Jahan Malek Khatun
  Faces of Love
    trans. by Dick Davis
    Deluxe 9780143107286

O'BRIEN, FLANN
  At Swim-Two-Birds
    PMC 9780141182681

O'CASEY, SEAN
  Cock-a-Doodle Dandy
  in *The Playboy of the Western World and Two Other Irish Plays*
    (see also J. M. Synge & W. B. Yeats)
    PC 9780140188783

O'CONNOR, FRANK
  The Genius
    Archive 9780241746998

My Oedipus Complex and Other Stories
    PMC 9780141187877

OH JUNG-HEE
Chinatown
    trans. by Bruce Fulton & Ju-Chan Fulton
    NS 9780241744369

OKAKURA, KAKUZO
The Book of Tea
    PC 9780141191843; LBC 9780241251355

OLIPHANT, MARGARET
Miss Marjoribanks
    PC 9780140436303

On Writing History from Herodotus to Herodian
    trans. by John Marincola
    PC 9780141393575

One Hundred Poets, One Poem Each: A Treasury of Classical Japanese Verse
    trans. by Peter MacMillan
    PC 9780141395937

ORCZY, BARONESS
The Scarlet Pimpernel
    PEL 9780241341339

ORIGO, IRIS
The Merchant of Prato: Daily Life in a Medieval Italian City
PMC 9780241293928

Orkneyinga Saga: The History of the Earls of Orkney
trans. by Hermann Pálsson & Paul Edwards
PC 9780140443837

OROZBAQ UULU, SAGHÏMBAY
The Memorial Feast for Kökötöy Khan: A Kirghiz Epic Poem in the Manas Tradition
trans. by Daniel Prior
PC 9780241544211

ORWELL, GEORGE
Animal Farm
PMC 9780141182704; Clothbound 9780241453865; PEL 9780241341667; NS 9780141393056; Student 9780241706985
Animal Farm: Illustrated Edition
PMC 9780241196687
Animal Farm: The Graphic Novel
illus. by Odyr
NS 9780241391853
Books v. Cigarettes
Great Ideas 9780141036618

Burmese Days
    PMC 9780141185378; NS 9780141395432
Can Socialists be Happy?
    Archive 9780241746905
A Clergyman's Daughter
    PMC 9780141184654
Coming Up for Air
    PMC 9780141185699
The Complete Novels of George Orwell
    PMC 9780141190396
Decline of the English Murder
    Great Ideas 9780141191263
Down and Out in Paris and London
    PMC 9780141184388; NS 9780141393032
Essays
    PMC 9780141183060; NS 9780141395463
Fascism and Democracy
    NS 9780241455678
Homage to Catalonia
    PMC 9780141183053; NS 9780141393025
Keep the Aspidistra Flying
    PMC 9780141183725; NS 9780141395470
A Life in Letters
    PMC 9780141192635
The Lion and the Unicorn: Socialism and the English Genius
    PMC 9780241315682

Nineteen Eighty-Four
    PC 9780241416419; PMC 9780141187761;
    Clothbound 9780241453513; PEL 9780241341650;
    NS 9780141393049; Student 9780241705407
Nineteen Eighty-Four: Anniversary Edition
    PMC 9780141191201
Nineteen Eighty-Four: The Graphic Novel
    illus. by Fido Nesti
    HB 9780241436493
Notes on Nationalism
    PM 9780241339565
Orwell and Politics
    ed. by Peter Davison
    PC 9780241417980
Orwell and the Dispossessed
    ed. by Peter Davison
    PC 9780241418000
The Orwell Diaries
    PMC 9780141191546
Orwell in Spain
    ed. by Peter Davison
    PC 9780241418017
Orwell's England
    ed. by Peter Davison
    PC 9780241418024
Politics and the English Language
    NS 9780141393063

The Road to Wigan Pier
  PMC 9780141185293; NS 9780141395456
Seeing Things as They Are: Selected Journalism and Other Writings
  PMC 9780141984230
Shooting an Elephant
  PMC 9780141187396; LCC 9780241630099
Some Thoughts on the Common Toad
  Great Ideas 9780141191270
Why I Write
  Great Ideas 9780141019000

OUOLOGUEM, YAMBO
Bound to Violence
  trans. by Ralph Manheim
  PMC 9780241680803

OVID
The Erotic Poems
  trans. by Peter Green
  PC 9780140443608
The Fall of Icarus
  trans. by Mary M. Innes
  LBC 9780141398679
Fasti
  trans. by A. J. Boyke & R. D. Woodard
  PC 9780140446906

Heroides
    trans. by Harold Isbell
    PC 9780140423556

Metamorphoses
    trans. by Arthur Golding
    PC 9780140422306
    trans. by Mary M. Innes
    PC 9780140440584
    trans. by David Raeburn
    PC 9780140447897; Clothbound 9780141394619
    trans. by Stephanie McCarter
    HB 9780525505990

OWEN, ROBERT

A New View of Society and Other Writings
    PC 9780140433487

OWEN, WILFRED

Anthem For Doomed Youth
    LBC 9780141397603

Poems
    Clothbound Poetry 9780241303115

Three Poets of the First World War
with Ivor Gurney & Isaac Rosenberg
    PC 9780141182070

P

PAINE, THOMAS
Common Sense
PC 9780140390162; Great Ideas 9780141018904
Rights of Man
PC 9780140390155
Thomas Paine Reader
PC 9780140444964

PARDO BAZÁN, EMILIA
The House of Ulloa
trans. by Paul O'Prey & Lucia Graves
PC 9780141392950
The Lady Bandit
trans. by Robert M. Fedorchek
Archive 9780241752111

PARKER, DOROTHY
Big Blonde
LCC 9780241609934
The Collected Dorothy Parker
PMC 9780141182582

Complete Poems
    PC 9780143106081
The Custard Heart
    PM 9780241339589
Horsie
    Archive 9780241747322

PASCAL, BLAISE
Human Happiness
    trans. by A. J. Krailsheimer
    Great Ideas 9780141036793
Pensées
    trans. by A. J. Krailsheimer
    PC 9780140446456

PATTEN, BRIAN
    with Adrian Henri & Roger McGough
The Mersey Sound
    PMC 9780141189260

PAUSANIAS
Guide to Greece
    trans. by Peter Levi
    Volume I: Central Greece
    PC 9780140442250
    Volume II: Southern Greece
    PC 9780140442267

PAVEL, OTA
How I Came to Know Fish
trans. by Jindriska Badal & Robert McDowell
PMC 9780141192833; Archive 9780241752289

PAVESE, CESARE
The House on the Hill
trans. by Tim Parks
PMC 9780241370520
The Moon and the Bonfires
trans. by Tim Parks
PMC 9780241370544

PAZ, OCTAVIO
The Labyrinth of Solitude
trans. by Lysander Kemp, Yara Milos & Rachel Phillips Belash
PMC 9780141188478

The Penguin Anthology of Classical Arabic Literature
ed. by Robert Irwin
PC 9780141441887

The Penguin Book of Bengali Short Stories
ed. by Arunava Sinha
HB 9780241562635

The Penguin Book of Caribbean Verse in English
ed. by Kasia Boddy
PC 9780140424607

The Penguin Book of Christmas Stories from Hans Christian Andersen to Angela Carter
   ed. by Jessica Harrison
   PC 9780241396704; Clothbound 9780241455654

The Penguin Book of Demons
   ed. by Scott G. Bruce
   PC 9780143137863

The Penguin Book of Dragons
   ed. by Scott G. Bruce
   PC 9780143135043

The Penguin Book of Dutch Short Stories
   ed. by Joost Zwagerman
   PMC 9780141395722

The Penguin Book of Elegy: Poems of Memory, Mourning and Consolation
   ed. by Andrew Motion & Stephen Regan
   PC 9780241269626

The Penguin Book of English Song: Seven Centuries of Poetry From Chaucer to Auden
   ed. by Richard Stokes
   PC 9780141982540

The Penguin Book of English Verse
   ed. by Paul Keegan
   PC 9780140424546

The Penguin Book of Existentialist Philosophy
    ed. by Jonathan Webber
    PC 9780241645413

The Penguin Book of Exorcisms
    ed. by Joseph P. Laycock
    PC 9780143135470

The Penguin Book of Feminist Writing
    ed. by Hannah Dawson
    PC 9780241633977

The Penguin Book of First World War Poetry
    ed. by Matthew George Walter
    PC 9780141181905

The Penguin Book of First World War Stories
    ed. by Barbara Korte & Ann-Marie Einhaus
    PC 9780141442150

The Penguin Book of French Poetry 1820–1950
    trans. by William Rees
    PC 9780140423853

The Penguin Book of French Short Stories
  Volume 1: From Marguerite de Navarre to Marcel Proust
    ed. by Patrick McGuinness
    PC 9780241462003
  Volume 2: From Colette to Marie NDiaye
    ed. by Patrick McGuinness
    PMC 9780241462065

The Penguin Book of Ghost Stories from Elizabeth Gaskell to Ambrose Bierce
    ed. by Newton, Michael
    PC 9780141442365

The Penguin Book of Greek and Latin Lyric Verse
    trans. by Christopher Childers
    PC 9780141392134

The Penguin Book of Haiku
    trans. by Adam L. Kern
    PC 9780140424768

The Penguin Book of Hebrew Verse
    trans. by T. Carmi
    PC 9780140424676

The Penguin Book of Hell
    ed. by Scott G. Bruce
    PC 9780143131625

The Penguin Book of Irish Poetry
    ed. by Patrick Crotty
    PC 9780141191645

The Penguin Book of Italian Short Stories
    ed. by Jhumpa Lahiri
    PC 9780241299852

The Penguin Book of Japanese Short Stories
    ed. by Jay Rubin
    PC 9780241311905

The Penguin Book of Japanese Verse from the Earliest Times to the Present
    trans. by Geoffrey Bownas & Anthony Thwaite
    PC 9780141190945

The Penguin Book of Korean Short Stories
    ed. by Bruce Fulton
    PC 9780241448519

The Penguin Book of Mermaids
    ed. by Cristina Bacchilega & Marie Alohalani Brown
    PC 9780143133728

The Penguin Book of Migration Literature
    ed. by Dohra Ahmad
    PC 9780143133384

The Penguin Book of Modern African Poetry
    ed. by Gerald Moore & Ulli Beier
    PC 9780140424720

The Penguin Book of Murder Mysteries
    ed. by Michael Sims
    PC 9780143137535

The Penguin Book of Oulipo
    ed. by Philip Terry
    PMC 9780241378458

The Penguin Book of Outer Space Exploration: NASA and the Incredible Story of Human Spaceflight
    ed. by John Logsdon
    PC 9780143129950

The Penguin Book of Pirates
    ed. by Katherine Howe
    PC 9780143137511

The Penguin Book of Polish Short Stories
    ed. by Antonia Lloyd-Jones
    HB 9780241563397

The Penguin Book of Renaissance Verse 1509–1659
    ed. by David Norbrook & H. R. Woudhuysen
    PC 9780140423464

The Penguin Book of Romantic Poetry
    ed. by Jonathan & Jessica Wordsworth
    PC 9780140435689

The Penguin Book of Russian Poetry
    ed. by Robert Chandler, Boris Dralyuk & Irina Mashinski
    PC 9780141198309

The Penguin Book of Scottish Verse
    ed. by Robert Crawford & Mick Imlah
    PC 9780140424669

The Penguin Book of Spanish Short Stories
    ed. by Margaret Jull Costa
    PC 9780241390504

The Penguin Book of Spiritual Verse: 110 Poets on the Divine
    ed. by Kaveh Akbar
    PC 9780241391594

The Penguin Book Of The British Short Story
  Volume 1: From Daniel Defoe to John Buchan
    ed. by Philip Hensher
    PC 9780141396002
  Volume 2: From P. G. Wodehouse to Zadie Smith
    ed. by Philip Hensher
    PMC 9780141396026

The Penguin Book of the Prose Poem from Baudelaire to Anne Carson
    ed. by Jeremy Noel-Tod
    PC 9780141984568

The Penguin Book of the Undead
    ed. by Scott G. Bruce
    PC 9780143107682

The Penguin Book of Victorian Verse
    ed. by Daniel Karlin
    PC 9780140445787

The Penguin Book of Witches
    ed. by Katherine Howe
    PC 9780143106180

Penguin's Poems by Heart
    ed. by Laura Barber
    PC 9780141191775

Penguin's Poems for Life
    ed. by Laura Barber
    PC 9780140424706; HB 9780713999617

Penguin's Poems for Love
    ed. by Laura Barber
    PC 9780140424805

Penguin's Poems for Weddings
    ed. by Laura Barber
    PC 9780141394701

PEPYS, SAMUEL
  The Diary of Samuel Pepys: A Selection
    PC 9780141439938
  The Great Fire of London
    LBC 9780141397542

PEREC, GEORGES
Brief Notes on the Art and Manner of Arranging One's Books
trans. by John Sturrock
Great Ideas 9780241475218
Species of Spaces and Other Pieces
trans. by John Sturrock
PC 9780141442242

PERRAULT, CHARLES
The Fairy Tales of Charles Perrault
trans. by Angela Carter
PMC 9780141189956

PERSIUS
Satires
in *The Satires of Horace and Persius*
trans. by Niall Rudd
(see also Horace)
PC 9780140455083

PESSOA, FERNANDO
The Book of Disquiet
trans. by Richard Zenith
PMC 9780241200131
I Have More Souls Than One
trans. by Jonathan Griffin
PM 9780241339602

A Little Larger Than the Entire Universe: Selected Poems
    trans. by Richard Zenith
    PC 9780143039556
Selected Poems
    trans. by Jonathan Griffin
    PMC 9780141184333

PETRARCH
Canzoniere
    trans. by Anthony Mortimer
    PC 9780140448160
Petrarch in English
    ed. by Thomas Roche
    PC 9780140434484

PETRONIUS
The Satyricon
    trans. by J. P. Sullivan
    PC 9780140448054

PETRUSHEVSKAYA, LUDMILLA
There Once Lived a Girl Who Seduced Her Sister's Husband, And He Hanged Himself: Love Stories
    trans. by Anna Summers
    PMC 9780141198583

There Once Lived a Mother Who Loved Her Children,
   Until They Moved Back In: Three Novellas About Family
   trans. by Anna Summers
   PMC 9780141198590

There Once Lived a Woman Who Tried to Kill Her
   Neighbour's Baby: Scary Fairy Tales
   trans. by Keith Gessen & Anna Summers
   PMC 9780718192075

The Philokalia: A Selection
   trans. by Andrew Louth & Jonathan L. Zecher
   PC 9780241201374

PINDAR
The Odes of Pindar
   trans. by Cecil Bowra
   PC 9780140442090

PIRANDELLO, LUIGI
Six Characters in Search of an Author and Other Plays
   trans. by Mark Musa
   PMC 9780140189223

PLATO
Early Socratic Dialogues
   trans. by Trevor J. Saunders, Iain Lane, Donald Watt & Robin Waterfield
   PC 9780140455038

Gorgias
    trans. by Walter Hamilton, rev. Chris Emlyn-Jones
    PC 9780140449044

The Last Days of Socrates
    trans. by Hugh Tredennick & Harold Tarrant
    PC 9780140449280
    trans. by Christopher Rowe
    PC 9780140455496

The Laws
    trans. by Trevor J. Saunders
    PC 9780140449846

Phaedrus
    trans. by Christopher Rowe
    PC 9780140449747

Philebus
    trans. by Robin Waterfield
    PC 9780140443950

Protagoras and Meno
    trans. by Adam Beresford
    PC 9780140449037

Republic
    trans. by Desmond Lee, rev. Melissa Lane
    PC 9780140455113
    trans. by Christopher Rowe
    PC 9780141442433

Socrates' Defence
   trans. by Christopher Rowe
   LBC 9780141397641
The Symposium
   trans. by Christopher Gill
   PC 9780140449273; Great Ideas 9780141023847
Theaetetus
   trans. by Robin Waterfield
   PC 9780140444506
Timaeus and Critias
   trans. by Desmond Lee
   PC 9780140455045
see also *Classical Literary Criticism*

PLAUTUS
The Pot of Gold and Other Plays
   trans. by E. F. Watling
   PC 9780140441499
The Rope and Other Plays
   trans. by E. F. Watling
   PC 9780140441369
see also *Classical Comedy*

PLINY THE ELDER
Natural History
   trans. by John F. Healy
   PC 9780140444131

PLINY THE YOUNGER
: *The Letters of the Younger Pliny*
  : trans. by Betty Radice
  : PC 9780140441277

PLOTINUS
: *The Enneads*
  : trans. by Stephen MacKenna
  : PC 9780140445206

PLUNKET, ROBERT
: *Love Junkie*
  : PMC 9780241795095
  : *My Search for Warren Harding*
  : PMC 9780241707999

PLUTARCH
: *The Age of Alexander*
  : trans. by Ian Scott-Kilvert, rev. Timothy E. Duff
  : PC 9780140449358
  : *Essays*
  : trans. by Robin Waterfield
  : PC 9780140445640
  : *Fall of the Roman Republic*
  : trans. by Rex Warner, rev. Robin Seager
  : PC 9780140449341
  : *The Makers of Rome*
  : trans. by Ian Scott-Kilvert
  : PC 9780140441581

On Sparta
    trans. by Richard J. A. Talbert
    PC 9780140449433
The Rise and Fall of Athens
    trans. by John Marincola & Ian Scott-Kilvert
    PC 9780140449051
The Rise of Rome
    trans. by Ian Scott-Kilvert, Jeffrey Tatum &
    Christopher Pelling
    PC 9780140449754
Rome in Crisis
    trans. by Ian Scott-Kilvert, rev. Christopher
    Pelling
    PC 9780140449167

POE, EDGAR ALLAN
The Fall of the House of Usher and Other Writings
    PC 9780141439815; Clothbound 9780241739846
Hop-Frog
    Archive 9780241746714
The Masque of the Red Death
    LCC 9780241573754
A Modern Detective
    LBC 9780241252321
The Murders in the Rue Morgue and Other Tales
    PEL 9780141198972

The Narrative of Arthur Gordon Pym of Nantucket
    PC 9780140437485
The Pit and the Pendulum
    PC 9780141190624
The Portable Edgar Allan Poe
    PC 9780143039914
The Raven
    HB 9780143122364
The Science Fiction of Edgar Allan Poe
    PC 9780140431063
The Tell-Tale Heart
    LBC 9780141397269

The Poem of the Cid: A Bilingual Edition with Parallel Text
    trans. by Rita Hamilkton & Janet Perry
    PC 9780140444469

Poems of the Great War 1914–1918
    NS 9780141181035

Poetry of the Thirties from Auden to Spender
    ed. by Robin Skelton
    PMC 9780141184579

A Poet's Guide to Britain
    ed. by Owen Sheers
    PC 9780141192840

POLANYI, KARL
The Great Transformation: The Political and Economic Origins of Our Time
PMC 9780241685556

POLIDORI, JOHN
The Vampyre
LBC 9780241776254

POLLAN, MICHAEL
Food Rules
Green 9780141997025

POLO, MARCO
The Travels
trans. by Nigel Cliff
PC 9780241253052; Clothbound 9780141198774

POLYBIUS
The Rise of the Roman Empire
trans. by Ian Scott-Kilvert
PC 9780140443622

POPE, ALEXANDER
The Rape of the Lock and Other Major Writings
PC 9780140423501

The Portable Beat Reader
ed. by Ann Charters
PC 9780142437537

The Portable Nineteenth-Century African American Women Writers
    ed. by Hollis Robbins & Henry Louis Gates, Jr.
    PC 9780143105992

PORTER, KATHERINE ANNE
Pale Horse, Pale Rider: Selected Short Stories
    PMC 9780141195315

POTOCKI, JAN
The Manuscript Found in Saragossa
    trans. by Ian Maclean
    PC 9780140445800

POTOK, CHAIM
The Chosen
    PMC 9780141040776
My Name is Asher Lev
    PMC 9780141190563

POWYS, JOHN COWPER
Wolf Solent
    PMC 9780241763018

PRATCHETT, TERRY
Night Watch
    PMC 9780241759011

The Pre-Raphaelites from Rossetti to Ruskin
    ed. by Dinah Roe
    PC 9780141192406

PRÉVOST, ABBÉ
Manon Lescaut
    trans. by Leonard Tancock, rev. Jean Sgard
    PC 9780140445596

PRICE, ANTHONY
The Labyrinth Makers
    Crime 9780241692387
Other Paths to Glory
    Crime 9780241661505

PRIESTLEY, J. B.
An Inspector Calls and Other Plays
    PMC 9780141185354

PRINCE, MARY
The History of Mary Prince
    PC 9780140437492

PROCOPIUS
The Secret History
    trans. by G. A. Williamson, rev. Peter Sarris
    PC 9780140455281

PROUST, MARCEL
- *Days of Reading*
  - trans. by John Sturrock
  - Great Ideas 9780141036731
- *In Search of Lost Time*
  - *Volume 1: The Way by Swann's*
  - trans. by Lydia Davis
  - PMC 9780141180311
  - *Volume 2: In the Shadow of Young Girls in Flower*
  - trans. by James Grieve
  - PMC 9780141180328
  - *Volume 3: The Guermantes Way*
  - trans. by Mark Treharne
  - PMC 9780141180335
  - *Volume 4: Sodom and Gomorrah*
  - trans. by John Sturrock
  - PMC 9780141180342
  - *Volume 5: The Prisoner* and *The Fugitive*
  - trans. by Carol Clark & Peter Collier
  - PMC 9780141180359
  - *Volume 6: Finding Time Again*
  - trans. by Ian Patterson
  - PMC 9780141180366
- *Remembrance of Things Past*
  - trans. by C. K. Scott Moncrieff
  - *Volume 1*
  - PC 9780241610510; Clothbound 9780241719688

Volume 2
PC 9780241610527; Clothbound 9780241719695
Volume 3 (trans. with Stephen Hudson)
PC 9780241610534; Clothbound 9780241719701

PSELLUS, MICHAEL
Fourteen Byzantine Rulers
trans. by E. R. A. Sewter
PC 9780140441697

PU SONGLING
Strange Tales from a Chinese Studio
trans. by John Minford
PC 9780140447408

PULLMAN, PHILIP
Grimm Tales for Young and Old
(see also the Brothers Grimm)
PC 9780141442228; Clothbound 9780241472729

PUSHKIN, ALEXANDER
Eugene Onegin
trans. by Stanley Mitchell
PC 9780140448108
Novels, Tales, Journeys
trans. by Richard Pevear & Larissa Volokhonsky
PC 9780241290378

The Queen of Spades
    trans. by Richard Pevear & Larissa Volokhonsky
    LCC 9780241573761
The Queen of Spades and Other Stories
    trans. by Rosemary Edmonds
    PC 9780140441192
Selected Poetry
    trans. by Antony Wood
    PC 9780241207130
Tales of Belkin and Other Prose Writings
    trans. by Ronald Wilks
    PC 9780140446753

Q

QIAN ZHONGSHU
Fortress Besieged
   trans. by Jeanne Kelly & Nathan K. Mao
   PMC 9780141187860

QU YUAN
The Songs of the South: An Ancient Chinese Anthology of Poems by Qu Yuan and Other Poets
   trans. by David Hawkes
   PC 9780141198705

QUENEAU, RAYMOND
Zazie in the Metro
   trans. by Barbara Wright
   PMC 9780241618875

QUEVEDO, FRANCISCO DE
  The Swindler
  in *Lazarillo de Tormes and The Swindler: Two Spanish Picaresque Novels*
    trans. by Michael Alpert
    PC 9780140449006

The Qur'an
  see *The Koran*

R

RABELAIS, FRANÇOIS
Gargantua and Pantagruel
trans. by M. A. Screech
PC 9780140445503

RACINE, JEAN
Iphigenia, Phaedra and Athaliah
trans. by John Cairncross
PC 9780140441222
see also *Four French Plays*

RADCLIFFE, ANN
The Italian
PC 9780140437546
The Mysteries of Udolpho
PC 9780140437591

RADIGUET, RAYMOND
The Devil in the Flesh
trans. by Robert Baldick
PC 9780241372616

Rama the Steadfast: An Early Form of the Ramayana
    trans. by John Brockington & Mary Brockington
    PC 9780140447446

The Ramayana: A Shortened Modern Prose Version of the Indian Epic
    trans. by R. K. Narayan
    PC 9780143039679

RAMPO, EDOGAWA
  Beast in the Shadows
    trans. by Ian Hughes
    Crime 9780241656914
  The Black Lizard
    trans. by Ian Hughes
    Crime 9780241645826
  Gold Mask
    trans. by William Varteresian
    Crime 9780241687369

RAND, AYN
  Anthem
    PMC 9780141189611
  Atlas Shrugged
    PMC 9780141188935
  The Fountainhead
    PMC 9780141188621

We the Living
    PMC 9780141193885

RAY, MAN
Self-Portrait
    PMC 9780141195506

REED, ISHMAEL
Flight to Canada
    PMC 9780241315194
Mumbo Jumbo
    PMC 9780241305812

REED, JOHN
Ten Days That Shook the World
    PC 9780141442129

REIMANN, BRIGITTE
Siblings
    trans. by Lucy Jones
    PMC 9780241555842
Woman in the Pillory
    trans. by Lucy Jones
    PMC 9780241718971

REIN, HEINZ
Berlin Finale
    trans. by Shaun Whiteside
    PMC 9780241245590

REYMONT, WŁADYSŁAW
The Peasants
trans. by Anna Zaranko
PC 9780241524244

REZZORI, GREGOR VON
The Snows of Yesteryear
trans. by H. F. Broch de Rothermann
PMC 9780141192734

RHYS, JEAN
After Leaving Mr Mackenzie
PMC 9780141183947
The Collected Short Stories
PMC 9780141984858
Good Morning, Midnight
PMC 9780141183930
Quartet
PMC 9780141183923
Smile Please
PMC 9780141984544
Voyage in the Dark
PMC 9780141183954
Wide Sargasso Sea
PMC 9780141182858; PMC 9780141185422;
Clothbound 9780241281901

RICHARDSON, SAMUEL
   Clarissa, or, The History of a Young Lady
      PC 9780140432152
   Pamela
      PC 9780140431407

The Rig Veda
      trans. by Wendy Doniger
      PC 9780140449891

RILKE, RAINER MARIA
   Letters to a Young Poet
      trans. by Charlie Louth
      PC 9780141192321; LCC 9780241620038;
      LBC 9780241252055
   The Notebooks of Malte Laurids Brigge
      trans. by Michael Hulse
      PC 9780141182216
   Selected Poems
      trans. by J. B. Leishman
      PMC 9780141183497

RIMBAUD, ARTHUR
   Selected Poems and Letters
      trans. by Jeremy Harding & John Sturrock
      PC 9780140448023

RIZAL, JOSÉ
Noli Me Tangere (Touch Me Not)
trans. by Harold Augenbraum
PC 9780143039693

ROBINSON, CEDRIC J.
Black Marxism: The Making of the Black Radical Tradition
PMC 9780241514177

ROCHÉ, HENRI-PIERRE
Jules et Jim
trans. by Patrick Evans
PMC 9780141194639

ROCHESTER, THE EARL OF
Selected Works
PC 9780140424591

Romantic Fairy Tales
trans. by Carol Tully
PC 9780140447323

ROMITA, SR., JOHN
with Joe Simon, Jack Kirby, Stan Lee & Jim Steranko
Captain America
Marvel 9780143135753; Marvel HB 9780143135746

RONSARD, PIERRE
Selected Poems
trans. by Malcolm Quainton & Elizabeth Vinestock
PC 9780140424249

Roots of Yoga
trans. by James Mallinson & Mark Singleton
PC 9780241253045

ROSE, GILLIAN
Love's Work
PMC 9780241645499

ROSENBERG, GÖRAN
Israel: A Personal History
trans. by Göran Rosenberg
PMC 9780241795712

ROSENBERG, ISAAC
with Ivor Gurney & Wilfred Owen
Three Poets of the First World War
PC 9780141182070

ROSSETTI, CHRISTINA
Complete Poems
PC 9780140423662
Goblin Market and Other Poems
Clothbound Poetry 9780241303061

Selected Poems
    PC 9780140424690
To Read and Dream
    Archive 9780241747230
see also *The Pre-Raphaelites*

ROSTAND, EDMOND
Cyrano de Bergerac
    trans. by Carol Clark
    PC 9780140449686

ROTH, HENRY
Call it Sleep
    PMC 9780141188652

ROTH, JOSEPH
The Radetzky March
    trans. by Joachim Neugroschel
    PMC 9780141393421

ROTH, WERNER
with Stan Lee, Jack Kirby, Roy Thomas, Don Heck & Neal Adams
X-Men
    Marvel 9780143135777; Marvel HB 9780143135760

ROUSSEAU, JEAN-JACQUES
- *The Body Politic*
  - trans. by Quintin Hoare
  - LBC 9780241252017
- *The Confessions*
  - trans. by J. M. Cohen
  - PC 9780140440331
- *A Discourse on Inequality*
  - trans. by Maurice Cranston
  - PC 9780140444391
- *Émile, or, On Education*
  - trans. by Allan Bloom
  - PC 9780140445633
- *Reveries of the Solitary Walker*
  - trans. by Peter France
  - PC 9780140443639
- *The Social Contract*
  - trans. by Maurice Cranston
  - PC 9780140442014; Great Ideas 9780141018881
- *Of the Social Contract and Other Political Writings*
  - trans. by Quintin Hoare
  - PC 9780141191751

RUMI
- *Selected Poems*
  - trans. by Coleman Banks, John Moyne, A. J. Arberry & Reynold Nicholson
  - PC 9780140449532

Where Everything is Music
    trans. by Coleman Banks & John Moyne
    Archive 9780241752364
Spiritual Verses: The First Book of the Masnavi-Ye Ma'navi
    trans. by Alan Williams
    PC 9780140447910

RUNCIMAN, STEVEN
A History of the Crusades
    Volume I: The First Crusades
    PMC 9780141985503
    Volume II: The Kingdom of Jerusalem
    PMC 9780241298763
    Volume III: The Kingdom of Acre
    PMC 9780241298770

RUNYON, DAMON
Guys and Dolls and Other Stories
    PMC 9780141188331
On Broadway
    PMC 9780141184234

RUSKIN, JOHN
The Lamp of Memory
    Great Ideas 9780141036670
On Art and Life
    Great Ideas 9780141018959

Unto This Last and Other Writings
PC 9780140432114

RUSSELL, RAY
The Case Against Satan
PC 9780143107279
Haunted Castles
PC 9780143129318

Russian Émigré Short Stories from Bunin to Yanovsky
ed. by Bryan Karetnyk
PC 9780241299739

Russian Magic Tales from Pushkin to Platonov
ed. by Robert Chandler
PC 9780141442235

Russian Short Stories from Pushkin to Buida
ed. by Robert Chandler
PC 9780140448467

RYLE, GILBERT
The Concept of Mind
PMC 9780141182179

S

SABATO, ERNESTO
On Heroes and Tombs
trans. by Helen R. Lane
PMC 9780141985862
The Tunnel
trans. by Margaret Sayers Peden
PMC 9780141194547

SACHER-MASOCH, LEOPOLD VON
Venus in Furs
trans. by Joachim Neugroschel
PC 9780140447811

The Saga of Grettir the Strong
trans. by Bernard Scudder
PC 9780140447736

The Saga of King Hrolf Kraki
trans. by Jesse L. Byock
PC 9780140435931

The Saga of the People of Laxardal and *Bolli Bollason's Tale*
    trans. by Keneva Kunz
    PC 9780140447750

The Saga of the Volsungs
    trans. by Jesse L. Byock
    PC 9780140447385; NS 9780141393681

SAGAN, FRANÇOISE
  Bonjour Tristesse
    trans. by Heather Lloyd
    LCC 9780241630891
  Bonjour Tristesse and *A Certain Smile*
    trans. by Heather Lloyd
    PMC 9780141198750

Sagas of Warrior-Poets
    ed. by Diana Whaley
    PC 9780140447712

SAHNI, BHISHAM
  Tamas
    trans. by Daisy Rockwell
    PC 9780143138051

SAID, EDWARD W.
  Orientalism
    PMC 9780141187426

SAINT-EXUPÉRY, ANTOINE DE
Flight to Arras
trans. by William Rees
PMC 9780141183183
The Little Prince
trans. by T. V. F. Cuffe
PMC 9780141185620; Clothbound 9780241508664
Night Flight
trans. by Curtis Cate & T. V. F. Cuffe
Archive 9780241747025
Southern Mail / Night Flight
trans. by Curtis Cate
PMC 9780141183749
Wind, Sand and Stars
trans. by William Rees
PMC 9780141183190

SAKI
The Complete Short Stories
PMC 9780141184494
Reginald's Christmas Revel
LCC 9780241597026

SALIH, TAYEB
   Season of Migration to the North
      trans. by Denys Johnson-Davies
      PMC 9780141187204

SALLUST
   Catiline's War, The Jugurthine War, Histories
      trans. by A. J. Woodman
      PC 9780140449488

SALTER, JAMES
   The Hunters
      PMC 9780141188645
   Light Years
      PMC 9780141188638
   Solo Faces
      PMC 9780141189581

SANCHEZ, SONIA
   This Is Not a Small Voice: Selected Poems
      PMC 9780241756041

SAPIENZA, GOLIARDA
   The Art of Joy
      trans. by Anne Milano Appel
      PMC 9780141198477

SAPPHO
: *Come Close*
  : trans. by Aaron Poochigian
  : LBC 9780141398693
: *Stung with Love: Poems and Fragments*
  : trans. by Aaron Poochigian
  : PC 9780140455571

SARASHINA, LADY
: *As I Crossed a Bridge of Dreams: Recollections of a Woman in Eleventh-Century Japan*
  : trans. by Ivan Morris
  : PC 9780140442823

SARTRE, JEAN-PAUL
: *The Age of Reason*
  : trans. by Eric Sutton
  : PMC 9780141185286
: *Huis Clos and Other Plays*
  : trans. by Kitty Black & Stuart Gilbert
  : PMC 9780141184555
: *Iron in the Soul*
  : trans. by Eric Sutton
  : PMC 9780141186573
: *Modern Times: Selected Non-Fiction*
  : trans. by Robin Buss
  : PMC 9780140189216

Nausea
    trans. by Robert Baldick
    PMC 9780141185491
The Reprieve
    trans. by Eric Sutton
    PMC 9780141185781
Words
    trans. by Irene Clephane
    PMC 9780141183466

SCHILLER, FRIEDRICH
Mary Stuart
    trans. by F. J. Lamport
    PC 9780140447118
On the Aesthetic Education of Man
    trans. by Keith Tribe
    PC 9780141396965
The Robbers and *Wallenstein*
    trans. by F. J. Lamport
    PC 9780140443684

SCHLOSSER, ERIC
Fast Food Nation: What The All-American Meal is Doing to the World
    PMC 9780241766064

SCHNEIDER, PETER
The Wall Jumper
trans. by Leigh Hafrey
PMC 9780141187983

SCHNITZLER, ARTHUR
A Confirmed Bachelor
trans. by E. C. Slade
Archive 9780241746790
Dream Story
trans. by J. M. Q. Davies
PMC 9780141182247; LCC 9780241620229

SCHOPENHAUER, ARTHUR
Essays and Aphorisms
trans. by R. J. Hollingdale
PC 9780140442274; Pocket HB 9780141395913
The Horrors and Absurdities of Religion
trans. by R. J. Hollingdale
Great Ideas 9780141191591
On the Suffering of the World
trans. by R. J. Hollingdale
Great Ideas 9780141018942

SCHREINER, OLIVE
The Story of an African Farm
PC 9780140431841

SCHUYLER, GEORGE S.
Black Empire
PC 9780143137078
Black No More
Sci-Fi 9780241505724

A Science Fiction Omnibus
ed. by Brian Aldiss
PMC 9780141188928

SCOTT, WALTER
Chronicles of the Canongate
PC 9780140439892
Guy Mannering
PC 9780140436570
The Heart of Mid-Lothian
PC 9780140431292
Ivanhoe
PC 9780140436587; PEL 9780141199139
Kenilworth
PC 9780140436549
Rob Roy
PC 9780140435542
Waverley
PC 9780140436600

Scottish Folk and Fairy Tales from Burns to Buchan
    ed. by Gordon Jarvie
    PC 9780141442266

SEACOLE, MARY
Wonderful Adventures of Mrs Seacole in Many Lands
    PC 9780140439021

SEARLE, RONALD
with Geoffrey Willans
Molesworth
    PMC 9780141186009

SEBASTIAN, MIHAIL
For Two Thousand Years
    trans. by Philip Ó Ceallaigh
    PMC 9780241189610

The Secret History of the Mongols
    trans. by Christopher P. Atwood
    PC 9780241197912

SEI SHŌNAGON, LADY
A Lady in Kyoto
    trans. by Meredith McKinney
    Archive 9780241752081
The Pillow Book
    trans. by Meredith McKinney
    PC 9780140448061

SELBY JR., HUBERT
The Demon
PMC 9780141195643
Last Exit to Brooklyn
PMC 9780141195650
Requiem for a Dream
PMC 9780141195667
The Room
PMC 9780141195674
Song of the Silent Snow
PMC 9780241951248
Waiting Period
PMC 9780141195681
The Willow Tree
PMC 9780141195698

Selections from the Carmina Burana
trans. by David Parlett
PC 9780140444407

SELVON, SAM
Calypso in London
LCC 9780241630877
The Housing Lark
PMC 9780241441329
The Lonely Londoners
PMC 9780141188416; Clothbound 9780241504123

Moses Ascending
   PMC 9780241504390
Ways of Sunlight
   PMC 9780241654538

SENECA
   Dialogues and Letters
      trans. by C. D. N. Costa
      PC 9780140446791
   Four Tragedies and Octavia
      (*Thyestes, Phaedra, The Trojan Women, Oedipus, Octavia*)
      trans. by E. F. Watling
      PC 9780140441741
   Letters from a Stoic
      trans. by Robin Alexander Campbell
      PC 9780140442106; Pocket HB 9780141395852
   On the Shortness of Life
      trans. by C. D. N. Costa
      Great Ideas 9780141018812
   Phaedra and Other Plays
      (*Hercules Insane, Trojan Women, Phaedra, Oedipus, Thyestes, Octavia*)
      trans. by R. Scott Smith
      PC 9780140455519

Why I am a Stoic
   trans. by Robin Alexander Campbell
   Archive 9780241746899
see also *How To Be a Stoic*

Seven Viking Romances
   trans. by Hermann Pálsson & Paul Edwards
   PC 9780140444742

SEWELL, ANNA
Black Beauty
   Deluxe 9780143106470

SEXTON, ANNE
Mercies: Selected Poems
   PMC 9780241460399

SHACKLETON, ERNEST
South: The Endurance *Expedition*
   PMC 9780241251096

SHAFFER, PETER
Amadeus
   PMC 9780141188898
Equus
   PMC 9780141188904
The Royal Hunt of the Sun
   PMC 9780141188881

SHAKESPEARE, WILLIAM

All's Well That Ends Well
  PC 9780141396262
Antony and Cleopatra
  PC 9780141396293
As You Like It
  PC 9780141396279
The Comedy of Errors
  PC 9780141396286
Coriolanus
  PC 9780141396453
Cymbeline
  PC 9780141396484
Four Comedies
  (*The Taming of the Shrew, A Midsummer Night's Dream, As You Like it, Twelfth Night*)
  PC 9780140434545
Four Histories
  (*Richard II, Henry IV Parts One & Two, Henry V*)
  PC 9780140434507
Four Tragedies
  (*Hamlet, Othello, King Lear, Macbeth*)
  PC 9780140434583; Clothbound 9780241726976
Hamlet
  PC 9780141396507
  see also *Five Revenge Tragedies*

Henry IV Part One
PC 9780141396682
Henry IV Part Two
PC 9780141396699
Henry V
PC 9780141396675
Henry VI Part One
PC 9780141396606
Henry VI Part Two
PC 9780141396408
Henry VI Part Three
PC 9780141396613
Henry VIII
PC 9780141396620
Is This a Dagger Which I See Before Me?
LBC 9780241252192
Julius Caesar
PC 9780141396538
King John
PC 9780141396521
King Lear
PC 9780141396460
Love's Labour's Lost
PC 9780141396439
Macbeth
PC 9780141396316

Measure for Measure
   PC 9780141396552
The Merchant of Venice
   PC 9780141396545
The Merry Wives of Windsor
   PC 9780141396576
A Midsummer Night's Dream
   PC 9780141396668
Much Ado About Nothing
   PC 9780141396590
Othello
   PC 9780141396514
Pericles
   PC 9780141396637
Richard II
   PC 9780141396644
Richard III
   PC 9780141396651
Romeo and Juliet
   PC 9780141396477
Shakespeare's Sonnets
   NS 9780141396224
The Sonnets and *A Lover's Complaint*
   PC 9780140436846; Clothbound 9780141192574
The Taming of the Shrew
   PC 9780141396583

The Tempest
  PC 9780141396309
Timon of Athens
  PC 9780141396491
Titus Andronicus
  PC 9780141396323
Troilus and Cressida
  PC 9780141396415
Twelfth Night
  PC 9780141396446
The Two Gentlemen of Verona
  PC 9780141396422
The Two Noble Kinsmen
  PC 9780241200568
The Winter's Tale
  PC 9780141396569

SHALAMOV, VARLAN
Kolyma Tales
  trans. by John Glad
  PMC 9780140186956

SHAW, GEORGE BERNARD
Androcles and the Lion
  PC 9780140450132
Back to Methuselah
  PC 9780140450149

The Doctor's Dilemma
  PC 9780140450279
Heartbreak House
  PC 9780140437874
John Bull's Other Island
  PC 9780140450446
Last Plays
  (*In Good King Charles's Golden Days, Buoyant Billions, Farfetched Fables, Shakes Versus Shav, Why She Would Not*)
  PC 9780140450422
Major Barbara
  PC 9780140437904
Man and Superman
  PC 9780140437881
Misalliance and *The Fascinating Foundling*
  PC 9780140450415
Plays Extravagant
  (*Too True to be Good, The Simpleton of the Unexpected Isles, The Millionairess*)
  PC 9780140450316
Plays Pleasant
  (*Arms and the Man, Candida, The Man of Destiny, You Never Can Tell*)
  PC 9780140437942

Plays Political
  (*The Apple Cart, On the Rocks, Geneva*)
  PC 9780140450309
Plays Unpleasant
  (*Widowers' Houses, The Philanderer, Mrs Warren's Profession*)
  PC 9780140437935
Pygmalion
  PC 9780141439501
Saint Joan
  PC 9780140437911
Selected Short Plays
  PC 9780140450248
Three Plays for Puritans
  (*The Devil's Disciple, Caesar and Cleopatra, Captain Brassbound's Conversion*)
  PC 9780140437928

SHECKLEY, ROBERT
  Dimension of Miracles
    Sci-Fi 9780241472491
  Untouched by Human Hands
    Sci-Fi 9780241473023

SHELLEY, MARY

Frankenstein

PC 9780141439471; Clothbound 9780141393391; HB 9780143122333; PEL 9780141198965; Deluxe 9780143105039

see also *Three Gothic Novels*

Frankenstein: The 1818 Text

PC 9780143131847

The Last Man

PC 9780143137900

Matilda

in *Mary* and *Maria, Matilda*

(see also Mary Wollstonecraft)

PC 9780140433715; LBC 9780241251874

Transformation

Archive 9780241746820

SHELLEY, PERCY BYSSHE

Selected Poems and Prose

PC 9780241253069

SHEN FU

Six Records of a Floating Life

trans. by Leonard Pratt & Chiang Su-hui

PC 9780140444292

SHERIDAN, RICHARD
The School for Scandal and Other Plays
PC 9780140432404

SHERRIFF, R. C.
The Hopkins Manuscript
PMC 9780241349076
Journey's End
PMC 9780141183268

SHIEL, M. P.
The Purple Cloud
PC 9780141196428

SHOLOKHOV, MIKHAIL
And Quiet Flows the Don
trans. by Stephen Garry
PMC 9780241284407

SIBURAPHA
Behind the Painting
trans. by David Smyth
PMC 9780241694466

SIDNEY, MARY
with Aemilia Lanyer & Isabella Whitney
Renaissance Women Poets
PC 9780140424096

SIDNEY, PHILIP
: *The Countess of Pembroke's Arcadia*
: PC 9780140431117
: *Sidney's 'The Defence of Poesy' and Selected Renaissance Literary Criticism*
: ed. by Gavin Alexander
: PC 9780141439389

SILKO, LESLIE MARMON
: *Ceremony*
: PMC 9780241441640

SIMENON, GEORGES
: *Betty*
: trans. by Ros Schwartz
: PMC 9780241487082
: *The Blue Room*
: trans. by Linda Coverdale
: PMC 9780141399041
: *The Carter of 'La Providence'*
: trans. by David Coward
: IM 9780141393469; MCC 9780241788165
: *The Cat*
: trans. by Ros Schwartz
: Demy 9780241808030
: *Cécile is Dead*
: trans. by Anthea Bell
: IM 9780141397054

The Cellars of the Majestic
　　trans. by Howard Curtis
　　IM 9780241188446
A Crime in Holland
　　trans. by Siân Reynolds
　　IM 9780141393490
The Dancer at the Gai-Moulin
　　trans. by Siân Reynolds
　　IM 9780141393520
Death Threats and Other Stories
　　trans. by Ros Schwartz
　　PMC 9780241487075
Félicie
　　trans. by David Coward
　　IM 9780241188668
The Flemish House
　　trans. by Shaun Whiteside
　　IM 9780141394770
The Grand Banks Café
　　trans. by David Coward
　　IM 9780141393506
The Hand
　　trans. by Linda Coverdale
　　PMC 9780241284650
The Hand and Other Novels
　　trans. by Linda Coverdale & Ros Schwartz
　　PMC 9780241787915

The Hanged Man of Saint-Pholien
    trans. by Linda Coverdale
    IM 9780141393452
The Hatter's Ghosts
    trans. by Howard Curtis
    PMC 9780241545386
Inspector Cadaver
    trans. by William Hobson
    IM 9780241188477
The Judge's House
    trans. by Howard Curtis
    IM 9780241188453
The Krull House
    trans. by Howard Curtis
    PMC 9780241453414
The Late Monsieur Gallet
    trans. by Anthea Bell
    IM 9780141393377
Liberty Bar
    trans. by David Watson
    IM 9780141396095
The Little Man from Archangel
    trans. by Siân Reynolds
    IM 9780241487068
Lock No. 1
    trans. by David Coward
    IM 9780141396101

Madame Maigret's Friend
    trans. by Howard Curtis
    IM 9780241240168
The Madman of Bergerac
    trans. by Ros Schwartz
    IM 9780141394565
The Mahé Circle
    trans. by Siân Reynolds
    PMC 9780141394169
Maigret
    trans. by Ros Schwartz
    IM 9780141397047
Maigret and Monsieur Charles
    trans. by Ros Schwartz
    IM 9780241304419
Maigret and the Dead Girl
    trans. by Howard Curtis
    IM 9780241297254
Maigret and the Ghost
    trans. by Ros Schwartz
    IM 9780241304037
Maigret and the Good People of Montparnasse
    trans. by Ros Schwartz
    IM 9780241303931

Maigret and the Headless Corpse
    trans. by Howard Curtis
    IM 9780241297261; MCC 9780241297261;
    Crime 9780241639245
Maigret and the Informer
    trans. by William Hobson
    IM 9780241304365
Maigret and the Killer
    trans. by Shaun Whiteside
    IM 9780241304266
Maigret and the Lazy Burglar
    trans. by Howard Curtis
    IM 9780241303917; MCC 9780241788233
Maigret and the Loner
    trans. by Howard Curtis
    IM 9780241304341
Maigret and the Man on the Bench
    trans. by David Watson
    IM 9780241277447
Maigret and the Minister
    trans. by Ros Schwartz
    IM 9780241279854
Maigret and the Nahour Case
    trans. by William Hobson
    IM 9780241304150

Maigret and the Old Lady
  trans. by Ros Schwartz
  IM 9780241206829
Maigret and the Old People
  trans. by Shaun Whiteside
  IM 9780241303894; MCC 9780241788288
Maigret and the Reluctant Witnesses
  trans. by William Hobson
  IM 9780241303856
Maigret and the Saturday Caller
  trans. by Siân Reynolds
  IM 9780241303955
Maigret and the Tall Woman
  trans. by David Watson
  IM 9780241277386
Maigret and the Tramp
  trans. by Howard Curtis
  IM 9780241303993
Maigret and the Wine Merchant
  trans. by Ros Schwartz
  IM 9780241304280
Maigret at Picratt's
  trans. by William Hobson
  IM 9780241240281
Maigret at the Coroner's
  trans. by Linda Coverdale
  IM 9780241206812

A Maigret Christmas and Other Stories
    trans. by David Coward
    PMC 9780241356746

Maigret Defends Himself
    trans. by Howard Curtis
    IM 9780241304068; MCC 9780241788196

Maigret Enjoys Himself
    trans. by David Watson
    IM 9780141985879

Maigret Gets Angry
    trans. by Ros Schwartz
    IM 9780141397320

Maigret Goes to School
    trans. by Linda Coverdale
    IM 9780241297575

Maigret Hesitates
    trans. by Howard Curtis
    IM 9780241304198

Maigret in Court
    trans. by Ros Schwartz
    IM 9780141985916

Maigret in New York
    trans. by Linda Coverdale
    IM 9780241206362

Maigret in Vichy
    trans. by Ros Schwartz
    IM 9780241304211; MCC 9780241788189

Maigret is Afraid
   trans. by Ros Schwartz
   IM 9780241277485

Maigret, Lognon and the Gangsters
   trans. by William Hobson
   IM 9780241250662

Maigret Sets a Trap
   trans. by Siân Reynolds
   IM 9780241297643; MCC 9780241788202

Maigret Takes a Room
   trans. by Shaun Whiteside
   IM 9780241206843

Maigret Travels
   trans. by Howard Curtis
   IM 9780241303825

Maigret's Anger
   trans. by William Hobson
   IM 9780241304013

Maigret's Childhood Friend
   trans. by Shaun Whiteside
   IM 9780241304235

Maigret's Dead Man
   trans. by David Coward
   IM 9780241206379; MCC 9780241788271

Maigret's Doubts
   trans. by Shaun Whiteside
   IM 9780141985893; MCC 9780241788219

Maigret's Failure
   trans. by William Hobson
   IM 9780241303788
Maigret's First Case
   trans. by Ros Schwartz
   IM 9780241206386
Maigret's Holiday
   trans. by Ros Schwartz
   IM 9780141980744; MCC 9780241788226
Maigret's Madwoman
   trans. by Siân Reynolds
   IM 9780241304303
Maigret's Memoirs
   trans. by Howard Curtis
   IM 9780241240175
Maigret's Mistake
   trans. by Howard Curtis
   IM 9780241279847
Maigret's Patience
   trans. by David Watson
   IM 9780241304136; MCC 9780241788240
Maigret's Pickpocket
   trans. by Siân Reynolds
   IM 9780241304174; MCC 9780241788172
Maigret's Revolver
   trans. by Siân Reynolds
   IM 9780241277430; Crime 9780241658970

Maigret's Secret
   trans. by David Watson
   IM 9780241303870
The Man from London
   trans. by Howard Curtis
   PMC 9780241461570
The Man Who Watched the Trains Go By
   trans. by Siân Reynolds
   PMC 9780241258552
A Man's Head
   trans. by David Coward
   IM 9780141393513
The Misty Harbour
   trans. by Linda Coverdale
   IM 9780141394794
Mr Hire's Engagement
   trans. by Anna Moschovakis
   PMC 9780141978468
My Friend Maigret
   trans. by Shaun Whiteside
   IM 9780241206393; LCC 9780241630792
The New Investigations of Inspector Maigret
   trans. by Howard Curtis & Ros Schwartz
   IM 9780241488546
Night at the Crossroads
   trans. by Linda Coverdale
   IM 9780141393483; Crime 9780241684771

The People Opposite
    trans. by Siân Reynolds
    PMC 9780241534724
Pietr the Latvian
    trans. by David Bellos
    IM 9780141392738
The Pitards
    trans. by David Bellos
    PMC 9780241325476
The Saint-Fiacre Affair
    trans. by Shaun Whiteside
    IM 9780141394756; MCC 9780241788257
The Shadow Puppet
    trans. by Ros Schwartz
    IM 9780141394183
Signed, Picpus
    trans. by David Coward
    IM 9780241188460
The Snow Was Dirty
    trans. by Howard Curtis
    PMC 9780241258569
Stan the Killer
    trans. by Ros Schwartz
    Archive 9780241752166
The Strangers in the House
    trans. by Howard Curtis
    PMC 9780241487099

Three Bedrooms in Manhattan
    trans. by Marc Romano & Lawrence G. Blochman
    PMC 9780241461563

The Two-Penny Bar
    trans. by David Watson
    IM 9780141394176

The Venice Train
    trans. by Ros Schwartz
    PMC 9780241544228

When I Was Old
    trans. by Helen Eustis
    PMC 9780241213131

The Yellow Dog
    trans. by Linda Asher
    IM 9780141393476

SIMON, JOE
    with Jack Kirby, Stan Lee, Jim Steranko, & John Romita Sr.
    Captain America
        Marvel 9780143135753; Marvel HB 9780143135746

SINCLAIR, UPTON
    The Jungle
        PC 9780140390315
    Oil!
        PC 9780143137443

SINGER, ISAAC BASHEVIS

Collected Stories
> trans. by Evelyn Torton Beck et al.
> PMC 9780141196770

Enemies: A Love Story
> trans. by Aliza Shevrin & Elizabeth Shub
> PMC 9780141197616

King of the Fields
> trans. by Isaac Bashevis Singer
> PMC 9780141391588

Love and Exile
> trans. by Joseph Singer
> PMC 9780141391595

The Magician of Lublin
> trans. by Elaine Gottlieb & Joseph Singer
> PMC 9780141197609

The Penitent
> trans. by Joseph Singer
> PMC 9780141391571

Shosha
> trans. by Joseph Singer
> PMC 9780141197630

The Slave
> trans. by Isaac Bashevis Singer & Cecil Hernley
> PMC 9780141197623

SINGER, PETER
  Why Vegan?
    Great Ideas 9780241472385

ŚIVADĀSA
  The Five-and-Twenty Tales of the Genie
    trans. by Chandra Rajan
    PC 9780140455199

ŠKVORECKÝ, JOSEF
  The Cowards
    trans. by Jeanne Němcová
    PMC 9780141047676

SMITH, ADAM
  The Invisible Hand
    Great Ideas 9780141036816
  The Theory of Moral Sentiments
    PC 9780143105923
  The Wealth of Nations
    Books I–III
    PC 9780140432084
    Books IV–V
    PC 9780140436150

SMITH, CLARK ASHTON
  The Dark Eidolon and Other Fantasies
    PC 9780143107385

SMITH, STEVIE
Selected Poems
PMC 9780141186559

SMOLLETT, TOBIAS
Humphry Clinker
PC 9780141441429
Roderick Random
PC 9780140433326

SOLOGUB, FYODOR
The Little Demon
trans. by Ronald Wilks
PC 9780141392936

SOLZHENITSYN, ALEXANDER
One Day in the Life of Ivan Denisovich
trans. by Ralph Parker
PMC 9780141184746

Some Men in London
Queer Life, 1945–1959
ed. by Peter Parker
HB 9780241370605
Queer Life, 1960–1967
ed. by Peter Parker
HB 9780241683705

The Song of Roland
    trans. by Glyn Burgess
    PC 9780140445329

The Songs of the South: An Ancient Chinese Anthology of Poems by Qu Yuan and Other Poets
    trans. by David Hawkes
    PC 9780141198705

SONTAG, SUSAN
  Against Interpretation and Other Essays
    PMC 9780141190068
  The Benefactor
    PMC 9780141190099
  Death Kit
    PMC 9780141393186
  Illness as Metaphor and *AIDS and Its Metaphors*
    PMC 9780141187129
  In America
    PMC 9780141190105
  Notes on Camp
    PM 9780241339701
  On Photography
    Design 9780141035789
  Styles of Radical Will
    PMC 9780141190051
  Under the Sign of Saturn
    PMC 9780141190082

The Volcano Lover
    PMC 9780141190112
Where the Stress Falls
    PMC 9780141190211

SOPHOCLES
Antigone
    trans. by Robert Fagles
    LBC 9780141397702
Electra and Other Plays
    (*Women of Trachis, Ajax, Electra, Philoctetes*)
    trans. by David Raeburn
    PC 9780140449785
The Three Theban Plays
    (*Antigone, Oedipus the King, Oedipus at Colonus*)
    trans. by E. F. Watling (as *The Theban Plays*)
    PC 9780140440034
    trans. by Robert Fagles
    PC 9780140444254
see also *Greek Tragedy*

SOROKIN, VLADIMIR
The Blizzard
    trans. by Jamey Gambrell
    PMC 9780241355138

Day of the Oprichnik
    trans. by Jamey Gambrell
    PMC 9780241355114

SŌSEKI, NATSUME
  Botchan
    trans. by J. Cohn
    PC 9780141391885; NS 9780241675281
  Kokoro
    trans. by Meredith McKinney
    PC 9780143106036
  Kusamakura
    trans. by Meredith McKinney
    PC 9780143105190
  Sanshirō
    trans. by Jay Rubin
    PC 9780140455625; Clothbound 9780241739839

SPARK, MURIEL
  The Ballad of Peckham Rye
    PMC 9780141188355
  The Driver's Seat
    PMC 9780141188348; Archive 9780241752036
  The Prime of Miss Jean Brodie
    PMC 9780141181424

Speaking of Śiva
    trans. by A. K. Ramanujan
    PC 9780140442700

SPENSER, EDMUND
The Faerie Queene
PC 9780140422078
The Shorter Poems
PC 9780140434453

SPINOZA, BENEDICT DE
Ethics
trans. by Edwin Curley
PC 9780140435719

STEGNER, WALLACE
All the Little Live Things
PMC 9780141392400
Angle of Repose
PMC 9780141188003
The Big Rock Candy Mountain
PMC 9780141392349
Collected Stories
PMC 9780141392387
Crossing to Safety
PMC 9780141394954
Recapitulation
PMC 9780141392394
A Shooting Star
PMC 9780141392356
The Spectator Bird
PMC 9780141392325

Wolf Willow
PMC 9780141392363

STEIN, GERTRUDE
The Autobiography of Alice B. Toklas
PMC 9780141185361
Food
PM 9780241339688
Paris France
Archive 9780241746806

STEINBECK, JOHN
The Acts of King Arthur and His Noble Knights
PMC 9780141186306
Burning Bright
PMC 9780141186061
Cannery Row
PMC 9780141185088
Cup of Gold
PMC 9780141186122
East of Eden
PMC 9780141185071; NS 9780141394893
The Grapes of Wrath
PMC 9780141185064; NS 9780141394886
In Dubious Battle
PMC 9780141186023
Journal of a Novel: The East of Eden Letters
PMC 9780141186344

A Life in Letters
   PMC 9780141186290
The Log from the Sea of Cortez
   PMC 9780141186078
The Long Valley
   PMC 9780141185514
The Moon is Down
   PMC 9780141185538
Of Mice and Men
   PMC 9780141185101; PMC 9780141023571;
   LCC 9780241620236; NS 9780141396033;
   Student 9780241670859
Once There Was a War
   PMC 9780141186320
The Pastures of Heaven
   PMC 9780141186092
The Pearl
   PMC 9780141185125; Clothbound 9780141394688;
   NS 9780141394909
The Red Pony
   PMC 9780141185095
A Russian Journal
   PMC 9780141186337
The Short Novels of John Steinbeck
   (*Tortilla Flat, The Moon is Down, The Red Pony,*
    Of Mice and Men, Cannery Row, The Pearl)
   Deluxe 9780143105770

The Short Reign of Pippin IV
  PMC 9780141186054
Sweet Thursday
  PMC 9780141185521
To a God Unknown
  PMC 9780141185507
Tortilla Flat
  PMC 9780141185118
Travels with Charley
  PMC 9780141186108
The Vigilante
  PM 9780241338957
The Wayward Bus
  PMC 9780141186115
The Winter of Our Discontent
  PMC 9780141186313
Zapata
  PMC 9780141186283

STENDHAL
  The Charterhouse of Parma
    trans. by John Sturrock
    PC 9780140449662
  The Life of Henry Brulard
    trans. by John Sturrock
    PC 9780140446111

Love
    trans. by Gilbert & Suzanne Sale
    PC 9780140443073
The Red and the Black
    trans. by Roger Gard
    PC 9780140447644

STERANKO, JIM
with Joe Simon, Jack Kirby, Stan Lee &
John Romita Sr.
Captain America
    Marvel 9780143135753; Marvel HB 9780143135746

STERNE, LAURENCE
The Life and Opinions of Tristram Shandy, Gentleman
    PC 9780141439778; Clothbound 9780241552667;
    PEL 9780141199993
A Sentimental Journey
    PC 9780140437799

STEVENSON, ROBERT LOUIS
An Apology for Idlers
    Great Ideas 9780141043968
The Black Arrow
    PC 9780141441399
In The South Seas
    PC 9780140434361
Kidnapped
    PC 9780141441795

The Master of Ballantrae
    PC 9780140434460
Selected Poems
    PC 9780140435481
The Strange Case of Dr Jekyll and Mr Hyde and Other Tales of Terror
    PC 9780141439730; Clothbound 9780241552681;
    PEL 9780141389509
Travels with a Donkey in the Cévennes and *The Amateur Emigrant*
    PC 9780141439464
Treasure Island
    PC 9780140437683; Clothbound 9780141192451
Treasure Island and *The Ebb-Tide*
    PEL 9780141199146

STOKER, BRAM
The Burial of the Rats
    Archive 9780241752272
Dracula
    PC 9780141439846; Clothbound 9780141196886;
    PEL 9780141199337; Deluxe 9780143106166
Dracula's Guest and Other Weird Tales
    PC 9780141441719

The Stonewall Reader
    ed. by Jason Baumann
    PC 9780143133513

The Story of Hong Gildong
    trans. by Minsoo Kang
   PC 9780143107699

STOWE, HARRIET
Uncle Tom's Cabin, or, Life Among the Lowly
   PC 9780140390032

STRACHEY, LYTTON
Eminent Victorians
   PMC 9780140183504

STRINDBERG, AUGUST
Three Plays
   (*The Father, Miss Julia, Easter*)
    trans. by Peter Watts
   PC 9780140440829

STRUGATSKY, ARKADY & BORIS
One Billion Years to the End of the World
    trans. by Antonina W. Bouis
   Sci-Fi 9780241472477

STURLUSON, SNORRI
King Harald's Saga
    trans. by Magnus Magnusson & Hermann Pálsson
   PC 9780140441833
The Prose Edda
    trans. by Jesse Byock
   PC 9780140447552; Archive 9780241752296

SUE, EUGÈNE
Mysteries of Paris
trans. by Carolyn Betensky & Jonathan Loesberg
PC 9780143107125

SUETONIUS
The Lives of the Caesars
trans. by Robert Graves (as *The Twelve Caesars*)
PC 9780140455168
trans. by Tom Holland
PC 9780141980386; HB 9780241186893

Suffragette Manifestos
Great Ideas 9780241472415

The Suffragettes
LBC 9780241252116

SUN TZU
The Art of War
trans. by John Minford
PC 9780143105756; Pocket HB 9780141395845;
Deluxe 9780140439199; Great Ideas 9780141023816;
NS 9780140455526

SUNDSTRÖM, GUN-BRITT
Engagement
trans. by Kathy Saranpa
Demy 9780241688120

SÜSKIND, PATRICK
Perfume: The Story of a Murderer
trans. by John E. Woods
PMC 9780241420294

SUSO, BAMBA
with Banna Kanute
Sunjata
trans. by Gordon Innes & Bakari Sidibe
PC 9780140447361

SVEVO, ITALO
Zeno's Conscience
trans. by William Weaver
PC 9780241372609

SWIFT, JONATHAN
Gulliver's Travels
PC 9780141439495; Clothbound 9780141196640;
PEL 9780141198989
A Modest Proposal
LBC 9780141398181
A Modest Proposal and Other Writings
PC 9780140436426

SWINBURNE, ALGERNON CHARLES
Poems and Ballads and *Atalanta in Calydon*
PC 9780140422504

SYMONS, A. J. A.
  The Quest for Corvo
    PMC 9780241312995

SYNGE, J. M.
  The Aran Islands
    PMC 9780140184327
  The Playboy of the Western World
  in *The Playboy of the Western World and Two Other Irish Plays*
    (see also Sean O'Casey & W. B. Yeats)
    PC 9780140188783

T

Ta Hsüeh and Chung Yung (The Highest Order of Cultivation and On the Practice of the Mean)
    trans. by Andrew Plaks
    PC 9780140447842

TABUCCHI, ANTONIO
Little Misunderstandings of No Importance and Other Stories
    trans. by Frances Frenaye
    PMC 9780241519288
Pereira Maintains: A Testimony
    trans. by Patrick Creagh
    PMC 9780241519301
Requiem: A Hallucination
    trans. by Margaret Jull Costa
    PMC 9780241519318; Archive 9780241752234

TACITUS
- *Agricola* and *Germania*
    trans. by Harold Mattingly, rev. S. A. Handford & J. B. Rives
    PC 9780140455403
- *Annals*
    trans. by Michael Grant (as *The Annals of Imperial Rome*)
    PC 9780140440607
    trans. by Cynthia Damon
    PC 9780140455649
- *The Histories*
    trans. by Kenneth Wellesley, rev. Rhiannon Ash
    PC 9780140449648

TAGORE, RABINDRANATH
- *The Broken Nest*
    trans. by Arunava Singh
    Archive 9780241752128
- *The Home and the World*
    trans. by Surendranath Tagore
    PC 9780140449860
- *Nationalism*
    Great Ideas 9780141192970
- *Selected Poems*
    trans. by William Radice
    PC 9780140449884

Selected Short Stories
    trans. by William Radice
    PC 9780140449839

The Táin
    trans. by Ciaran Carson
    PC 9780140455304

The Tale of Princess Fatima, Warrior Woman: The Arabic Epic of Dhat Al-Himma
    trans. by Melanie Magidow
    PC 9780143134268

The Tale of the Heike
    trans. by Royall Tyler
    PC 9780143107262

The Tales of Ise
    trans. by Peter MacMillan
    PC 9780141392578

Tales of the German Imagination from the Brothers Grimm to Ingeborg Bachmann
    trans. by Peter Wortsman
    PC 9780141198804

Tales of the Marvellous and News of the Strange
    trans. by Malcolm Lyons
    PC 9780241299951

Tales from the Thousand and One Nights
   see *The Arabian Nights*

TALESE, GAY
   Frank Sinatra Has a Cold and Other Essays
      PMC 9780141194158

The Talmud: A Selection
      trans. by Norman Solomon
      PC 9780141441788

TANPINAR, AHMET HAMDI
   The Time Regulation Institute
      trans. by Maureen Freely & Alexander Dawe
      PMC 9780141195759

TENNYSON, ALFRED LORD
   Idylls of the King
      PC 9780140422535
   Selected Poems
      PC 9780140424430

TERENCE
   The Comedies
      trans. by Betty Radice
      PC 9780140443240
   see also *Classical Comedy*

TERESA OF ÁVILA
The Life of Saint Teresa of Ávila by Herself
trans. by J. M. Cohen
PC 9780140440737

TESLA, NIKOLA
My Inventions and Other Writings
PC 9780143106616

TEY, JOSEPHINE
Brat Farrar
Crime 9780241658994
The Franchise Affair
Crime 9780241639139

THACKERAY, WILLIAM MAKEPEACE
The History of Henry Esmond
PC 9780140430493
The History of Pendennis
PC 9780140430769
Vanity Fair
PC 9780141439839; Clothbound 9780141199542; PEL 9780141199641

THEOGNIS
- *Elegies*
  in *Hesiod and Theognis*
    trans. by Dorothea Wender
    (see also Hesiod)
    PC 9780140442830

The Theory of the Modern Stage
    ed. by Eric Bentley
    PMC 9780141189185

THEROUX, PAUL
- *The Great Railway Bazaar*
    PMC 9780141189147
- *The Old Patagonian Express*
    PMC 9780141189154

THESIGER, WILFRED
- *Arabian Sands*
    PC 9780141442075
- *The Marsh Arabs*
    PC 9780141442082

THOMAS, DYLAN
- *A Child's Christmas in Wales*
    LCC 9780241790007
- *Do Not Go Gentle into That Good Night*
    Archive 9780241746264

Under Milk Wood: A Play for Voices
   PC 9780241636008

THOMAS, EDWARD
Selected Poems and Prose
   PC 9780141393193

THOMAS, R. S.
Selected Poems
   PMC 9780140188905

THOMAS, ROY
The Avengers
with Stan Lee, Jack Kirby, Don Heck, John Buscema & Sal Buscema
   Marvel 9780143135791; Marvel HB 9780143135784
X-Men
with Stan Lee, Jack Kirby, Werner Roth, Don Heck & Neal Adams
   Marvel 9780143135777; Marvel HB 9780143135760

THOMAS À KEMPIS
The Imitation of Christ
   trans. by Robert Jeffery
   PC 9780141191768

THOMAS OF BRITAIN
'Tristran'
in *Tristan with the 'Tristran' of Thomas*
trans. by A. T. Hatto
(see also Gottfried von Strassburg)
PC 9780140440980

THOMAS OF MONMOUTH
The Life and Passion of William of Norwich
trans. by Miri Rubin
PC 9780141197487

THOMPSON, E. P.
The Making of the English Working Class
PMC 9780141976952

THOMPSON, FLORA
Lark Rise to Candleford
(*Lark Rise, Over to Candleford, Candleford Green*)
PMC 9780141183312

THOMPSON, HUNTER S.
Fear and Loathing at Rolling Stone
PMC 9780241960417
Hell's Angels
PMC 9780141187457
Kingdom of Fear
PMC 9780241196496

THOREAU, HENRY DAVID
- *Walden* and *Civil Disobedience*
  PC 9780140390445
- *Where I Lived, and What I Lived For*
  Great Ideas 9780141023977
- *The Portable Thoreau*
  PC 9780143106500

Three Elizabethan Domestic Tragedies
  (*A Woman Killed with Kindness*, *Arden of Faversham*, *A Yorkshire Tragedy*)
  ed. by Keith Sturgess
  PC 9780141389813

Three Gothic Novels
  (*The Castle of Otranto*, *Vathek*, *Frankenstein*)
  PC 9780140430363

Three Japanese Buddhist Monks
  trans. by Meredith McKinney
  Great Ideas 9780241472910

Three Japanese Short Stories
  trans. by Jay Rubin
  PM 9780241339749

Three Restoration Comedies
  (*The Man of Mode*, *The Country Wife*, *Love for Love*)
    ed. by Gamini Salgado
    PC 9780140430271

Three Revenge Tragedies
  (*The Revenger's Tragedy*, *The White Devil*, *The Changeling*)
    ed. by Gamini Salgado
    PC 9780141441245

THUCYDIDES
History of the Peloponnesian War
    trans. by Rex Warner
    PC 9780140440393

THUNBERG, GRETA
No One Is Too Small to Make a Difference
    Green 9780241514573

THURBER, JAMES
The Secret Life of Walter Mitty
    PMC 9780241282618
The Thurber Carnival
    PMC 9780141395975

THURMAN, WALLACE
The Blacker the Berry
    PC 9780143131878

The Tibetan Book of the Dead
    trans. by Gyurme Dorje
    PC 9780140455267

TIPTREE JR., JAMES
Ten Thousand Light-Years from Home
    Sci-Fi 9780241469231
Warm Worlds and Otherwise
    Sci-Fi 9780241509753

Titanic: First Accounts
    ed. by Tim Maltin
    Deluxe 9780143106623

TOCQUEVILLE, ALEXIS DE
Ancien Régime and the Revolution
    trans. by Gerald E. Bevan
    PC 9780141441641
Democracy in America and *Two Essays on America*
    trans. by Gerald E. Bevan
    PC 9780140447606

TOLSTOY, LEO
Anna Karenina
    trans. by Richard Pevear & Larissa Volokhonsky
    PC 9780140449174; Clothbound 9780141199610
Childhood, Boyhood, Youth
    trans. by Judson Rosengrant
    PC 9780140449921

A Confession
    trans. by Jane Kentish
    Great Ideas 9780141036694

A Confession and Other Religious Writings
    trans. by Jane Kentish
    PC 9780140444735

The Cossacks
    trans. by David McDuff
    LCC 9780241573778

The Cossacks and Other Stories
    trans. by David McDuff
    PC 9780140449594

The Death of Ivan Ilyich
    trans. by Anthony Briggs
    LBC 9780241251768

The Death of Ivan Ilyich and Other Stories
    trans. by David McDuff, Ronald Wilks & Anthony Briggs
    PC 9780140449617

Family Happiness
    trans. by David McDuff
    Archive 9780241746936

How Much Land Does a Man Need?
    trans. by Ronald Wilks
    LBC 9780141397740

How Much Land Does a Man Need? and Other Stories
    trans. by Ronald Wilks
    PC 9780140445060

The Kreutzer Sonata and Other Stories
    trans. by Paul Foote & David McDuff
    PC 9780140449600

Last Steps: The Late Writings of Leo Tolstoy
    ed. by Jay Parini
    PC 9780141191195

Master and Man and Other Stories
    trans. by Paul Foote & Ronald Wilks
    PC 9780140449624

Resurrection
    trans. by Anthony Briggs
    PC 9780140424638

War and Peace
    trans. by Anthony Briggs
    PC 9780140447934; Clothbound 9780241265543

What is Art?
    trans. by Richard Pevear & Larissa Volokhonsky
    PC 9780140446425

TOOLE, JOHN KENNEDY
A Confederacy of Dunces
    PMC 9780141182865; Clothbound 9780241284667

TOOMER, JEAN
: *Cane*
: PC 9780143133674

Tottel's Miscellany: Songs and Sonnets of Henry Howard, Earl of Surrey, Sir Thomas Wyatt and Others
: ed. Amanda Holton & Tom MacFaul
: PC 9780141192048

TRANSTRÖMER, TOMAS
: *The Half-Finished Heaven: Selected Poems*
: trans. by Robert Bly
: PMC 9780241362822

Travels with a Writing Brush: Classical Japanese Travel Writing from the Manyōshū to Bashō
: trans. by Meredith McKinney
: PC 9780241310878

TRESSELL, ROBERT
: *The Ragged Trousered Philanthropists*
: PMC 9780141187693

TROLLOPE, ANTHONY
: *Christmas at Thompson Hall and Other Christmas Stories*
: HB 9780143122470
: *The Chronicles of Barsetshire*
: *The Warden*
: PC 9780140432145; PEL 9780141198996

Barchester Towers
PC 9780140432039
Doctor Thorne
PC 9780140433265
Framley Parsonage
PC 9780140432138
The Small House at Allington
PC 9780140433258
The Last Chronicle of Barset
PC 9780140437522
Dr Wortle's School
PC 9780140434040
He Knew He Was Right
PC 9780140433913
The Palliser Novels
    Can You Forgive Her?
    PC 9780140430868
    Phineas Finn
    PC 9780140430851
    The Eustace Diamonds
    PC 9780141441207
    Phineas Redux
    PC 9780140437621
    The Prime Minister
    PC 9780140433494
    The Duke's Children
    PC 9780140433449

The Way We Live Now
   PC 9780140433920

TROLLOPE, FANNY
Domestic Manners of the Americans
   PC 9780140435610

TROTSKY, LEON
History of the Russian Revolution
   trans. by Max Eastman
   PMC 9780241301319

TRUMBO, DALTON
Johnny Got His Gun
   PMC 9780141189819

TRUTH, SOJOURNER
Ain't I A Woman?
   Great Ideas 9780241472361

TSIANG, H. T.
The Hanging on Union Square
   PC 9780143134022

TSUSHIMA, YUKO
Child of Fortune
   trans. by Geraldine Harcourt
   PMC 9780241335031; NS 9780241675274

Of Dogs and Walls
    trans. by Geraldine Harcourt
    PM 9780241339787
Territory of Light
    trans. by Geraldine Harcourt
    PMC 9780241312629; LCC 9780241620243
Wildcat Dome
    trans. by Lisa Hofmann-Kuroda
    Demy 9780241649466

TU FU
    with Li Po
Poems
    trans. by Arthur Cooper
    PC 9780140442724

TURGENEV, IVAN
Fathers and Sons
    trans. by Peter Carson
    PC 9780141441337
First Love
    trans. by Isaiah Berlin
    PC 9780140443356
Home of the Gentry
    trans. by Richard Freeborn
    PC 9780140442243

On the Eve
   trans. by Gilbert Gardiner
   PC 9780140440096
Rudin
   trans. by Richard Freeborn
   PC 9780140443042
Sketches from a Hunter's Album
   trans. by Richard Freeborn
   PC 9780140445220
Spring Torrents
   trans. by Leonard Schapiro
   PC 9780140443691

TWAIN, MARK
   The Adventures of Huckleberry Finn
      PC 9780141439648; PC 9780143107323;
      Clothbound 9780141199573; PEL 9780141199009;
      Deluxe 9780143105947
   The Adventures of Tom Sawyer
      PC 9780143107330
   A Connecticut Yankee at King Arthur's Court
      PC 9780140430646
   Pudd'nhead Wilson
      PC 9780140430400

Roughing It
  PC 9780140390100
A Tramp Abroad
  PC 9780140436082

TYNDALE, WILLIAM
  The Obedience of a Christian Man
    PC 9780140434774

U

UNDSET, SIGRID
Kristin Lavransdatter
    trans. by Tiina Nunnally
    Deluxe 9780143039167

Unsung: Unheralded Narratives of American Slavery and Abolition
    ed. by the Schomburg Center for Research in Black Culture
    PC 9780143136088

The Upaniṣhads
    trans. by Juan Mascaró
    PC 9780140441635
    trans. by Valerie J. Roebuck
    PC 9780140447491

UPDIKE, JOHN
Brazil
    PMC 9780141188942

The Centaur
   PMC 9780141189048
The Complete Henry Bech
   PMC 9780141188560
The Coup
   PMC 9780141188959
Couples
   PMC 9780141188980
In the Beauty of the Lilies
   PMC 9780141188577
Marry Me
   PMC 9780141189406
Memories of the Ford Administration
   PMC 9780141188997
A Month of Sundays
   PMC 9780141189000
Of the Farm
   PMC 9780141189024
The Poorhouse Fair
   PMC 9780141188485
Rabbit at Rest
   PMC 9780141188447
Rabbit is Rich
   PMC 9780141188553
Rabbit Redux
   PMC 9780141188546

Rabbit, Run
 PMC 9780141187839
Roger's Version
 PMC 9780141188430
S.
 PMC 9780141189017
Toward the End of Time
 PMC 9780141188966
The Witches of Eastwick
 PMC 9780141188973

V

VAN GOGH, VINCENT
For Art and for Life
trans. by Arnold Pomerans
Archive 9780241752463
The Letters of Vincent Van Gogh
trans. by Arnold Pomerans
PC 9780140446746

VAN GULIK, ROBERT
The Chinese Gold Murders
Crime 9780241704646

VASARI, GIORGIO
Leonardo da Vinci
trans. by George Bull
LBC 9780141397764
Lives of the Artists
trans. by George Bull
Volume 1
PC 9780140445008

Volume 2
PC 9780140444605

VEBLEN, THORSTEIN
Conspicuous Consumption
　Great Ideas 9780141023984
The Theory of the Leisure Class
　PC 9780140187953

VERGA, GIOVANNI
Cavalleria Rusticana and Other Stories
　trans. by G. H. McWilliam
　PC 9780140447415

VERNE, JULES
Around the World in Eighty Days
　trans. by Michael Glencross
　PC 9780140449068; Clothbound 9780241468654;
　NS 9780141035871
Journey to the Centre of the Earth
　trans. by Frank Wynne
　PC 9780141441979
Twenty Thousand Leagues Under the Sea
　trans. by David Coward •
　PC 9780141394930; Clothbound 9780241198773

VESAAS, TARJEI
- *The Birds*
    - trans. by Torbjorn Støverud & Michael Barnes
    - PMC 9780241384879
- *The Ice Palace*
    - trans. by Elizabeth Rokkan
    - PMC 9780241321218

VICO, GIAMBATTISTA
- *New Science*
    - trans. by David Marsh
    - PC 9780140435696

VIGNY, ALFRED DE
- *The Warrior's Life*
    - trans. by Roger Gard
    - PC 9780141392806

VILLEHARDOUIN, GEOFFREY OF
with John of Joinville
- *Chronicles of the Crusades*
    - trans. by Caroline Smith
    - PC 9780140449983

The Vinland Sagas
- trans. by Keneva Kunz
- PC 9780140447767

VISNU ŚARMA
- *The Pañćatantra*
    - trans. by Chandra Rajan
    - PC 9780140455205

VIRGIL
- *The Aeneid*
    - trans. by John Dryden
    - PC 9780140446272
    - trans. by W. F. Jackson Knight
    - PC 9780140440515
    - trans. by David West
    - PC 9780140449327; Clothbound 9780141996332
    - trans. by Robert Fagles
    - PC 9780143106296; Deluxe 9780143105138
- *The Eclogues*
    - trans. by Guy Lee
    - PC 9780140444193
- *The Georgics*
    - trans. by L. P. Wilkinson
    - PC 9780140444148
    - trans. by Kimberly Johnson (as *The Georgics: A Poem of the Land*)
    - PC 9780140455632

VITRUVIUS
- *On Architecture*
  - trans. by Richard Schofield
  - PC 9780141441689

VOLTAIRE
- *Candide, or, Optimism*
  - trans. by Theo Cuffe
  - PC 9780140455106; Deluxe 9780143039426
- *Letters on England*
  - trans. by Leonard Tancock
  - PC 9780140443868
- *Micromégas and Other Short Fictions*
  - trans. by Theo Cuffe
  - PC 9780140446869
- *Miracles and Idolatry*
  - trans. by Theodore Besterman
  - Great Ideas 9780141023922
- *Philosophical Dictionary*
  - trans. by Theodore Besterman
  - PC 9780140442571
- *Treatise on Toleration*
  - trans. by Desmond M. Clarke
  - PC 9780241236628
- *Zadig* and *L'Ingénu*
  - trans. by John Butt
  - PC 9780140441260

VON ARNIM, ELIZABETH
Elizabeth and her German Garden
PEL 9780241341292
The Enchanted April
PMC 9780141191829; LCC 9780241619742

VONNEGUT, KURT
Cat's Cradle
PMC 9780141189345; Sci-Fi 9780241467985

W

WAGNER, RICHARD
The Ring of the Nibelung
trans. by John Deathridge
PC 9780241422281; Clothbound 9780241305850

WALLACE, ALFRED RUSSEL
The Malay Archipelago
PC 9780141394404

WALPOLE, HORACE
The Castle of Otranto
PC 9780140437676
see also *Three Gothic Novels*

WALSER, ROBERT
The Assistant
PMC 9780141189284

WANG WEI
Poems
trans. by G. W. Robinson
PC 9780141398419

WANG XIAOBO
- *Golden Age*
  - trans. by Yan Yan
  - PMC 9780241634226
- *The Maverick Pig*
  - trans. by Yan Yan
  - Archive 9780241747315
- *Pleasure of Thinking*
  - trans. by Yan Yan
  - PMC 9780241633267

WARHOL, ANDY
- *a*
  - PMC 9780241586402
- *The Andy Warhol Diaries*
  - ed. by Pat Hackett
  - PMC 9780141193076
- *Beauty*
  - Archive 9780241752326
- *Fame*
  - PM 9780241339800
- *The Philosophy of Andy Warhol*
  - PMC 9780141189109
- *POPism*
  - with Pat Hackett
  - PMC 9780141189420

WARNER, SYLVIA TOWNSEND
After the Death of Don Juan
PMC 9780241476079
The Corner That Held Them
PMC 9780241454817
The Flint Anchor
PMC 9780241476086
Lolly Willowes
PMC 9780241454886; LCC 9780241573785
Mr Fortune's Maggot
PMC 9780241476093
Summer Will Show
PMC 9780241454848
The True Heart
PMC 9780241476109

WARREN, ROBERT PENN
All the King's Men
PMC 9780141188614

WASSERMANN, JAKOB
My First Wife
trans. by Michael Hofmann
PMC 9780141391809

WAUGH, EVELYN
Black Mischief
PMC 9780141183985

Brideshead Revisited
   PMC 9780141182483; Clothbound 9780241284629;
   HB 9780241585313; PEL 9780241472736
The Complete Short Stories
   PMC 9780141193687
Decline and Fall
   PMC 9780141180908; HB 9780241585290
Edmund Campion: Jesuit and Martyr
   PMC 9780141391502
A Handful of Dust
   PMC 9780141183961; HB 9780241585276; PEL
   9780241341100
Helena
   PMC 9780140182439
Labels: A Mediterranean Journal
   PMC 9780140188370
The Letters of Nancy Mitford and Evelyn Waugh
with Nancy Mitford
   PMC 9780141193922
The Life of Right Reverend Ronald Knox
   PMC 9780141391519
A Little Learning: An Autobiography
   PMC 9780140183092
A Little Order
   PMC 9780141182933
The Loved One
   PMC 9780141184241

The Ordeal of Gilbert Pinfold
  PMC 9780141184500
Put Out More Flags
  PMC 9780141184012
Remote People
  PMC 9780141186399
Rossetti: His Life and Works
  PMC 9780241547885
Scoop
  PMC 9780141184029; HB 9780241585306
Sword of Honour
  (*Men at Arms, Officers and Gentlemen, Unconditional Surrender*)
  PMC 9780141184975; HB 9780241585320
  Men at Arms
  PMC 9780141185736
  Officers and Gentlemen
  PMC 9780141184678
  Unconditional Surrender
  PMC 9780141186870
Vile Bodies
  PMC 9780141182872; HB 9780241585283
Waugh in Abyssinia
  PMC 9780141185057
When the Going Was Good
  PMC 9780140182538

Work Suspended and Other Stories
    PMC 9780141184517

The Way of a Pilgrim: Candid Tales of a Wanderer to His Spiritual Father
    trans. by Anna Zaranko
    PC 9780241201350

WEBB, CHARLES
The Graduate
    PMC 9780141190242

WEBER, MAX
Protestant Ethic and the 'Spirit' of Capitalism and Other Writings
    trans. by Peter Baehr & Gordon C. Wells
    PC 9780140439212

WEBSTER, JOHN
The Duchess of Malfi and *The White Devil*
in *The Duchess of Malfi, The White Devil, The Broken Heart and 'Tis Pity She's a Whore*
    (see also John Ford)
    PC 9780141392233
Three Plays
    (*The White Devil, The Duchess of Malfi, The Devil's Law-Case*)
    PC 9780140430813
see also *Three Revenge Tragedies*

WEIL, SIMONE
- *The Need for Roots*
    - trans. by Ros Schwartz
    - PC 9780241467978
- *The Power of Words*
    - trans. by Richard Rees & Arthur Wills
    - Great Ideas 9780241472903
- *An Anthology*
    - ed. by Siân Miles
    - PMC 9780141188195

WELCH, DENTON
- *In Youth is Pleasure*
    - PC 9780241464137

WELLINGTON, THE DUKE OF
- *Military Dispatches*
    - PC 9780141394312

WELLS, H. G.
- *Ann Veronica*
    - PC 9780141441092
- *The Country of the Blind and Other Selected Stories*
    - PC 9780141441986
- *The First Men in the Moon*
    - PC 9780141441085

The Great Science Fiction
  (*The Time Machine*, *The Island of Doctor Moreau*, *The Invisible Man*, *The War of the Worlds*, *Short Stories*)
  PMC 9780241277492
The History of Mr Polly
  PC 9780141441078
The Invisible Man
  PC 9780141439983; PEL 9780141389516
The Island of Doctor Moreau
  PC 9780141441023; PEL 9780141389394
Kipps
  PC 9780141441108
Love and Mr Lewisham
  PC 9780141441054
A Modern Utopia
  PC 9780141441122
The New Machiavelli
  PC 9780141439990
The Shape of Things to Come
  PC 9780141441047
A Short History of the World
  PC 9780141441825
The Sleeper Awakes
  PC 9780141441061
The Time Machine
  PC 9780141439976; PEL 9780141199344;
  Archive 9780241746721

Tono-Bungay
    PC 9780141441115
The War in the Air
    PC 9780141441306
The War of the Worlds
    PC 9780141441030; Clothbound 9780241382707;
    PEL 9780141199047

WELLS, IDA
The Light of Truth
    PC 9780143106821

WELTY, EUDORA
The Golden Apples
    PMC 9780141196848

WERFEL, FRANZ
The Forty Days of Musa Dagh
    trans. by Geoffrey Dunlop, rev. James Reidel
    PMC 9780241332863

WEST, NATHANAEL
The Day of the Locust
    PEL 9780241341674
The Day of the Locust and *The Dream Life of Balso Snell*
    PMC 9780141182889

WHARTON, EDITH

The Age of Innocence
PC 9780140189704; PEL 9780241652688
The Custom of the Country
PC 9780143039709; Deluxe 9780143137214
Ethan Frome
PC 9780142437803; PEL 9780141389400
The House of Mirth
PC 9780140187298; PEL 9780141199023
Summer
PC 9780140186796; PC 9780241422243;
LCC 9780241630815
Three Novels of New York
(*The House of Mirth*, *The Custom of the Country*, *The Age of Innocence*)
Deluxe 9780143106555

WHITE, GILBERT

The Natural History of Selborne
PC 9780140431124

WHITMAN, WALT

The Complete Poems
PC 9780140424515
Leaves of Grass
PC 9780140421996;
Clothbound Poetry 9780241303122

On the Beach at Night Alone
  LBC 9780141398228

WHITNEY, ISABELLA
  with Aemilia Lanyer & Mary Sidney
  Renaissance Women Poets
    PC 9780140424096

Why Are We 'Artists'? 100 World Art Manifestos
    ed. by Jessica Lack
    PMC 9780241236314

WIESEL, ELIE
  Night
    trans. by Marion Wiesel
    PMC 9780140189896

WILDE, OSCAR
  The Ballad of Reading Gaol and Other Poems
    PC 9780141192673
  The Canterville Ghost, The Happy Prince and Other Stories
    NS 9780141192666
  The Complete Fairy Tales
    PEL 9780241770979
  The Complete Short Fiction
    PC 9780141439693
  De Profundis and Other Prison Writings
    PC 9780140439908

The Decay of Lying
   Great Ideas 9780241472453
The Decay of Lying and Other Essays
   PC 9780141192659
The Importance of Being Earnest and Other Plays
   PC 9780140436068
Lord Arthur Savile's Crime
   LBC 9780141397788
Nothing . . . Except My Genius: The Wit and Wisdom of Oscar Wilde
   NS 9780141192680
Only Dull People Are Brilliant at Breakfast
   LBC 9780241251805
The Picture of Dorian Gray
   PC 9780141439570; Clothbound 9780141442464;
   PEL 9780141199498; NS 9780141192642
A Poet Can Survive Everything But a Misprint
   Archive 9780241746738
The Soul of Man Under Socialism and Selected Critical Prose
   PC 9780140433876
The Star-Child
   LCC 9780241597033
see also *Decadent Poetry*

WILDER, THORNTON
The Bridge of San Luis Rey
PMC 9780141184258
Our Town and Other Plays
PMC 9780141184586

WILLANS, GEOFFREY
with Ronald Searle
Molesworth
PMC 9780141186009

WILLIAMS, ERIC
Capitalism and Slavery
PMC 9780241548165

WILLIAMS, TENNESSEE
Baby Doll and Other Plays
PMC 9780141190297
Cat on a Hot Tin Roof
PMC 9780141190280
The Glass Menagerie
PMC 9780141190266
Memoirs
PMC 9780141189291
Mister Paradise and Other One-Act Plays
PMC 9780141188423
The Rose Tattoo and Other Plays
PMC 9780141186504

A Streetcar Named Desire
 PMC 9780141190273
Suddenly Last Summer and Other Plays
 PMC 9780141191096
Sweet Bird of Youth and Other Plays
 PMC 9780141191089

WILLIAMS, WILLIAM CARLOS
Selected Poems
 PMC 9780141184340

WILLIAMSON, HENRY
Tarka the Otter
 PMC 9780141190358

WILLMOTT, PETER
with Michael Young
Family and Kinship in East London
 PMC 9780141189123

WILSON, EDWARD O.
Every Species is a Masterpiece
 Green 9780241514559

WILSON, SLOAN
The Man in the Gray Flannel Suit
 PMC 9780141188263

WINNICOTT, D. W.
The Child, the Family and the Outside World
PMC 9780241455685

WISNIEWSKI-SNERG, ADAM
Robot
trans. by Tomasz Mirkowicz
Sci-Fi 9780241485118

WITTGENSTEIN, LUDWIG
Tractatus Logico-Philosophicus
trans. by Alexander Booth
PC 9780241484173

WOLFE, THOMAS
Look Homeward, Angel
PMC 9780241215746
Of Time and the River
PMC 9780241215760

WOLLSTONECRAFT, MARY
Mary and *Maria*
in *Mary and Maria, Matilda*
(see also Mary Shelley)
PC 9780140433715

A Short Residence in Sweden
in *A Short Residence in Sweden and Memoirs of the Author of 'The Rights of Woman'*
  (see also William Godwin)
  PC 9780140432695
A Vindication of the Rights of Woman
  PC 9780141441252; Pocket HB 9780241382622;
  Great Ideas 9780141018911

Women in Power: Classical Myths and Stories from the Amazons to Cleopatra
  ed. by Stephanie McCarter
  PC 9780143136361

Women Who Did: Stories by Men and Women, 1890–1914
  ed. by Angelique Richardson
  PC 9780141441566

WOODSON, CARTER G.
The Mis-Education of the Negro
  PC 9780143137467

WOOLF, VIRGINIA
Between the Acts
  PC 9780241372500
Flush
  LBC 9780241251478
Jacob's Room
  PC 9780140185706

Mrs Dalloway
    PC 9780241371947; PMC 9780241436271;
    Clothbound 9780241468647; PEL 9780241341117
The New Dress
    Archive 9780241746967
Night and Day
    PC 9780140185683
Orlando
    PC 9780241371961; PMC 9780241436301;
    Clothbound 9780241284643; Deluxe 9780143138211
A Room of One's Own
    PMC 9780241436288; Pocket HB 9780141395920;
    Great Ideas 9780141018980
A Room of One's Own / Three Guineas
    PC 9780241371978
Selected Short Stories
    PC 9780241372517
Street Haunting
    LCC 9780241677100
To the Lighthouse
    PC 9780241371954; PMC 9780141183411; PEL
    9780241341681; Deluxe 9780143137580
The Voyage Out
    PC 9780140185638
The Waves
    PC 9780241372081; PMC 9780141182711

The Years
    PC 9780241372074

WOOLRICH, CORNELL
I Married a Dead Man
    Crime 9780241695869

WORDSWORTH, DOROTHY
with William Wordsworth
Home at Grasmere: Extracts from the Journal of Dorothy Wordsworth and from the Poems of William Wordsworth
    PC 9780140431360

WORDSWORTH, WILLIAM
A Life in Letters
    PC 9780141442136
Lyrical Ballads
with Samuel Taylor Coleridge
    PC 9780140424621; Clothbound Poetry 9780241303108
The Prelude: The Four Texts (1798, 1799, 1805, 1850)
    PC 9780140433692
Selected Poems
    PC 9780140424423

WRIGHT, JAY
>   *Transfigurations: Collected Poems*
>   PMC 9780241747421

Writings from Ancient Egypt
>   trans. by Toby Wilkinson
>   PC 9780141395951

Writings from the Zen Masters
>   trans. by Nyogen Senzaki & Paul Reps
>   Great Ideas 9780141043845

WU CH'ENG-EN
Monkey King: Journey to the West
>   trans. by Arthur Waley (as *Monkey*)
>   PC 9780140441116
>   trans. by Julia Lovell
>   PC 9780143138938; Clothbound 9780141393445
Monkey King Makes Havoc in Heaven
>   trans. by Julia Lovell
>   Archive 9780241752401

WYATT, THOMAS
The Complete Poems
>   PC 9780140422276
>   see also *Tottel's Miscellany*

WYNDHAM, JOHN
Chocky
PMC 9780141191492
The Chrysalids
PMC 9780141181479
The Day of the Triffids
PMC 9780141185415; Clothbound 9780241284674

X

X, MALCOLM
with Alex Haley
The Autobiography of Malcolm X
PMC 9780141185439

XENOPHON
Conversations of Socrates
trans. by Hugh Tredennick, rev. Robin Waterfield
PC 9780140445176
Hiero the Tyrant and Other Treatises
trans. by Robin Waterfield
PC 9780140455250
A History of My Times
trans. by Rex Warner
PC 9780140441758
The Persian Expedition
trans. by Rex Warner
PC 9780140440072

Y

YANAGI, SOETSU
The Beauty of Everyday Things
   trans. by Michael Brase
   Design 9780241366356

YEATS, W. B.
The Countess Cathleen
in *The Playboy of the Western World and Two Other Irish Plays*
   (see also J. M. Synge & Sean O'Casey)
   PC 9780140188783
Sailing to Byzantium
   Archive 9780241746981
Selected Plays
   PMC 9780140183740
Selected Poems
   PMC 9780141181257
A Terrible Beauty Is Born
   LBC 9780241251515

The Tower
   Clothbound Poetry 9780241303092
When You Are Old: Early Poems, Plays and Fairy Tales
   PC 9780143107644
Writings on Irish Folklore, Legend and Myth
   PMC 9780140180015

YEVTUSHENKO, YEVGENY
Selected Poems
   trans. by Robin Milner-Gulland & Peter Levi
   PC 9780140424775

YEZIERSKA, ANZIA
Bread Givers
   PC 9780143137719

YOUNG, MICHAEL
with Peter Willmott
Family and Kinship in East London
   PMC 9780141189123

YOURCENAR, MARGUERITE
Memoirs of Hadrian
   trans. by Grace Frick
   PMC 9780141184968

ZAMYATIN, YEVGENY
We
trans. by Clarence Brown
PC 9780140185850; Sci-Fi 9780241458747

ZOBEL, JOSEPH
Black Shack Alley
PC 9780143133957

ZOLA, ÉMILE
Au Bonheur des Dames (The Ladies' Delight)
trans. by Robin Buss
PC 9780140447835
The Beast Within
trans. by Roger Whitehouse
PC 9780140449631
The Debacle
trans. by Leonard Tancock
PC 9780140442809

The Drinking Den
    trans. by Robin Buss
    PC 9780140449549
The Earth
    trans. by Douglas Parmée
    PC 9780140443875
Germinal
    trans. by Roger Pearson
    PC 9780140447422
Nana
    trans. by George Holden
    PC 9780140442632
Thérèse Raquin
    trans. by Robin Buss
    PC 9780140449440

ZWEIG, STEFAN
Beware of Pity
    trans. by Jonathan Katz
    PMC 9780241678763
Chess
    trans. by Anthea Bell
    PMC 9780241305164; LCC 9780241630822;
    Archive 9780241747292
Six Stories
    trans. by Jonathan Katz
    PMC 9780141192826

100 Artists' Manifestos from the Futurists to the Stuckists
 ed. by Alex Danchev
 PMC 9780141191799